THOMAS C. NODDINGS is president of Thomas C. Noddings & Associates, Inc., a Chicago-based brokerage firm specializing in the research and execution of advanced investment strategies. Early in his investment career he developed an intense interest in convertibles, warrants and options. His conviction that these types of securities offered investors a profit potential superior to conventional stock purchases led him to do extensive research on the subject. As a result he has become an authority on the use of convertible securities and hedging strategies to realize above-average returns on investment capital.

Mr. Noddings is also the author of *How The Experts Beat The Market*, *The Dow Jones-Irwin Guide to Convertible Securities*, and a co-author of *Listed Call Options; Your Daily Guide to Portfolio Strategy*.

Thomas C. Noddings & Associates, Inc. was founded in 1977 to provide money management services to a growing number of serious investors throughout the country. The firm's ongoing research, supplemented by input from other hedging professionals, provides its clients with sophisticated investment techniques.

ADVANCED INVESTMENT STRATEGIES™

ADVANCED INVESTMENT STRATEGIES™

Thomas C. Noddings

Dow Jones-Irwin
Homewood, Illinois 60430

ISBN 0-87094-170-4
Library of Congress Catalog Card No. 78–62631

Printed in the United States of America

1 2 3 4 5 6 7 8 9 0 K 5 4 3 2 1 0 9 8

FOREWORD

These have been difficult years for most stock market investors. Taking inflation and taxes into account, most of us can show portfolio losses for the past *decade.* Institutions and individuals alike share the poor results. Over much longer periods than the recent past, studies seem to show low rates of return once all costs and inflation are fully considered; hardly encouraging news for a reader to encounter on the way into Tom Noddings' book on investing profitably. Yet the poor results most of us have "enjoyed" are factual. We need not be dyed-in-the-wool random walk adherents to appreciate the fact that most average investors holding a large number of portfolio positions over a few market cycles will achieve only *ordinary results* when *ordinary investing* techniques are employed.

Thus, we have to contend with the twin problems of the market's so-so long-term total rate of return as well as our inability to outperform the crowd. In this book, Mr. Noddings convincingly presents a group of investment strategies designed to produce superior results, improved total return, and above-average performance in all types of markets. Underlying these strategies are some basic concepts that should be understood.

First, risk must be managed so that large losses are avoided. It is only a matter of time before an average stock portfolio sinks by a third, requiring a 50 percent comeback to just break even! This book presents low-risk strategies that are designed to avoid disasters.

Second, in the nooks and crannies of the equity-related markets, there are various convertible securities that at times are either undervalued or overvalued relative to their underlying common stocks. These valuation inefficiencies create the investment opportunities we are constantly on the alert for.

Third, the principles of hedging overvalued and undervalued securities against each other and the desirability of doing so should also be appreciated. At this point, the reader will have advanced far beyond the knowledge level of millions of average investors. The author's hedging skills will be presented to you in detail.

Fourth, the Superhedge™ idea—that it is prudent and sensible to take long and short hedge positions in unrelated securities—should be chewed on, swallowed, and digested. We finally have the means for taking full advantage of market inefficiencies to our advantage. A good share of this book deals with the principles and practices of this unusual form of hedging.

These are insights and strategies far removed from the simple ownership of common stocks, and by far more valid than having a covered call portfolio at today's low option premiums. Understanding all that is set forth in this book will require hard work, but for those wishing to achieve the returns portrayed, with less risk than simple portfolios have, it will surely be worthwhile to put forth that effort.

Tom Noddings has the facility to make practical even the most complex hedging idea. Perhaps that's the final "dividend" for readers of this book. Not only will we discover what the advanced strategies are, we will be shown how to put the strategies to work. I had the fortunate insight to create and apply what is now called SUPERHEDGE™ I. But it was Tom Noddings who logically analyzed and presented it in a form that a reasonably sophisticated investor could understand and could consistently make use of. Tom has done the same with the other tools and strategies he has developed and perfected. Without a doubt, you will be a far-better equipped investor when you've mastered the contents of this book. By putting these strategies to work, you should be able to wisely and profitably invest as only a handful are now doing.

When I first started hedging (with Tom as my broker) I was unsure of myself. So I let him do all the work. Then when I conceived my first good hedge idea, he said, "Welcome to the club." To you as you start through this invaluable book, I'll also say, "Welcome to the club!"

August 1978   **Stanley Kritzik**

PREFACE

I could say this book was written for the serious investor who wants to earn an above average return in the stock market at below average risk. That's true, but it is also too simplistic. Most experienced investors who have developed their own investment guidelines over the years are reluctant to accept new ideas. This book, then, is not for them.

This book is for investors willing to approach the subject of modern portfolio management with open minds. They realize that times change. They also realize that, as in any other profession, gaining superior results requires a great deal of knowledge and expertise. These investors are willing to devote time and effort toward mastering new strategies and techniques.

My objective is to completely revise your approach to the stock market. For example, if you own any shares of common stock they should be sold immediately. There are far better investment instruments for today's stock market than common stock.

When I wrote *How the Experts Beat the Market* in 1976 I believed that it would be my last book on the subject of advanced investment strategies. I did not forsee the strategies we were employing so successfully at the time changing so dramatically. However, change they did so this new book had to be written.

The material in this book is the result of many years of in-depth research and actual investment experience and includes contributions from several investment professionals. I am especially indebted to Earl Zazove and to Stanley Kritzik, two exceptionally sophisticated investors.

Dr. Zazove, my coauthor of *Listed Call Options* published in 1975, made invaluable contributions during the countless hours of analysis and development of the concepts and strategies you are about to learn.

Stan Kritzik is the inventor of the Superhedge™—the most dynamic and potentially rewarding investment strategy available in today's stock market. Not only did he originate the idea, he also reduced it to a practical system that others may employ.

My thanks also to my partners, John Calamos, Carol Sachs, Don Mesler, and Connie Castanuela. Without their enthusiasm and support, it would not have been possible for me to make this book the comprehensive work that it is.

August 1978   **Thomas C. Noddings**

CONTENTS

MUST YOU SETTLE FOR A TIE IN TODAY'S STOCK MARKET?

You've often heard that the intelligent investor can beat the stock market by following a few simple rules. That is, in fact, what most investment books and advisory services are all about whether they are fundamentally or technically oriented. Why else would investors spend their money and their even more valuable time on such books or services?

Unfortunately, it just isn't that easy. Even full-time professional money managers who have access to information and resources far beyond those available to the individual investor are starting to "throw in the towel." These managers are yielding to the most current trend in money management, which is simply tying the market, rather than attempting to beat it.

The reason for this dramatic policy shift is that most professional money managers have been consistently *underperforming the stock market*. Confirming this fact, the March 21, 1977, issue of *Business Week* reported that bank-managed pension funds earned a shockingly low 1.1 percent annual return during the previous five years as compared with 4.9 percent by the *unmanaged* Standard & Poor's 500 stock index (dividends included for both). Going back ten years to include the "good old days of the late sixties" (1967 and 1968), the banks still underperformed the S&P 500 by nearly two percentage points annually.

During 1977, the popularity of secondary stocks and takeover candidates permitted many investors to beat the major indices like the S&P

500 which was down 7.2 percent (adjusted for dividends). However, most banks experienced continuing difficulties. The trust officer of a major Chicago bank, for example, seemed "proud" during a televised interview that his bank outperformed the Dow Jones Industrial Average in 1977 (who didn't?), although the bank's portfolio still *underperformed* the S&P by 3.2 percentage points.

Will 1978 be any better? It doesn't look that way! The blue chip and large growth stocks commonly held by the institutional money managers were the worst performers during the first half.

This poor performance by professional money managers is a most serious matter that cannot be swept under the rug by the financial community forever. It just won't go away as Wall Street and LaSalle Street firms would like to believe. What's more, the trustees of our nation's pension funds should not be expected to subsidize the financial community establishment via money management fees and brokerage commissions at the expense of either their pension fund contributors or their company profits.

A solution must be found, and the index fund concept is the one currently being bandied about most often in financial circles.

Indexing requires few management fees or trading expenses—one simply purchases all the stocks that make up the S&P 500 (or the Dow Jones, or whatever) and then holds them "forever." In other words, indexing gives up trying to win the game and concentrates rather on just going for the tie!

The trend toward indexing should not be taken lightly by the financial community. A look at the following statistics tells us why.

At the end of 1977, more than $4 billion had been switched from conventional money management funds to index funds, and it appears that substantially more money will follow. Assuming a 2-percent total annual expense figure for management fees and brokerage commissions for nonindexed portfolios, the financial community lost over $80 million in annual revenues. Placed in perspective, this $80 million revenue loss nearly equaled half the net profit of all New York Stock Exchange member firms for 1977.

Let's take a closer look at what indexing is all about by examining the first mutual fund to jump on the "indexing band wagon."

FIRST INDEX INVESTMENT TRUST

First Index Investment Trust, a no-load mutual fund and member of the Vanguard Group of Investment Companies, was established in 1976. Until First Index's entry into the market, indexing had been available only to the largest pension plans and other substantial investors.

First Index's 1977 annual report raises an interesting question: "Why settle for just average investment performance?" Their answer to the question they posed was: Although the S&P 500 is sometimes called a market *average,* its performance has been *well above average,* as indicated in a study by Becker Securities Corporation, the investment industry's major performance measurement service. The Becker study shows that the S&P 500 outperformed the common stock portfolios of 95 percent of the several thousand professionally managed pension funds measured for the 10-year period from 1967 through 1976. Thus, the performance of the Index is not average.

However, a close analysis of First Index Investment Trust's annual report reveals two interesting factors to consider. First, the fund's performance did not quite match the S&P 500 (−11.7% versus −11.5%). Although the report did not attempt to explain the negative 0.2 percent (no serious matter but I would still like to know why), an even more important difference existed. The losses for the year 1977, as First Index reported, were not adjusted for dividend income for either the S&P 500 or for First Index. Since the expenses incurred by the fund (mostly for administration and operations) exceeded 10 percent of the income received from their common stock investments (equal to about a 5-percent yield), the fund actually underperformed the S&P 500 by another ½ percent.

So, it's only right to include First Index Investment Trust with those professionally managed (or nonmanaged) funds that underperformed the market in 1977, and *for every year into the future!*

IS THERE AN ANSWER?

Through this book I offer no solutions to the problems facing trustees of the *large* pension funds and *I don't have any!* I raised the issue regarding First Index only to demonstrate how difficult it really is for anybody to beat the stock market and to provide a reference point for the superior investment strategies I will later present. These advanced strategies will permit *smaller* investors, both *individuals* and *pension funds,* to increase greatly the odds in their favor.

CAN YOU TIP THE ODDS IN YOUR FAVOR?

Considering the poor track records of the full-time professionals, do smaller investors have any reasonable chance of winning at the stock market game, or should they follow suit and settle for a "near tie" as indexing proponents suggest?

The answer must be obvious if you play by the same rules as the "pros." To compete with them on an equal basis requires a wealth of specialized knowledge, access to the best research available (inside information if you prefer), and unlimited time. That is what you need just to compete. To win is even tougher. But one fact remains very clear; you cannot expect to win if you're playing the game by their rules, and judging from past performances, chances are remote that you'll even come out with a tie.

The reason behind so much of this pessimistic news is that conventional approaches to investing are no longer profitable, much less prudent, in today's stock market. In fact, conventional approaches, believe it or not, have become dangerously speculative as holders of such blue chip stocks as Eastman Kodak, General Motors, and Xerox can verify. Even the all-American darling IBM has underperformed the market in recent years.

A brand new stock market exists today, and to make money in it, you need a new approach—a strategy that doesn't compete with the large institutions, but one that can actually *exploit* those investment opportunities that are simply not available to the "big money."

These opportunities are not in the area of speculative investments as one might easily assume. Rather, these opportunities include such blue chip investment instruments as convertible bonds on high-quality stocks, available simply because most convertible bonds lack the huge liquidity needed by institutional money managers in developing a portfolio. The opportunities I speak of also include specialized techniques where the institutions are restricted by the size of their capital or by government imposed regulations, e.g., put and call options and short selling. The institutions are usually restricted even where these tools are employed in the most conservative strategies as I will demonstrate later in this book.

In addition, any superior strategy must be one that is not extensively promoted by the brokerage community to its *retail* customers. By definition, the strategy must therefore be too difficult for the majority of brokers (or their customers) to comprehend or to employ effectively. Or the strategy must require too much time and effort relative to the commissions earned. Can you imagine stockbrokers attempting to explain such complex convertible bond features as conversion premium, investment floor, dilution protection, or call provisions to their hundreds of customers—and then earn but the usual modest commission (for bonds) if they were fortunate enough to make the sale? Of course not! They have to earn a living, too, which they do by providing the services *that their customers want*. It's much more reasonable to expect brokers to recommend a new issue of a utility stock or other conventional investments than to propose sophisticated strategies that their customers don't understand and won't appreciate.

And what about publishers of investment advisory services? As investment professionals, isn't it their responsibility to educate the public by providing the best possible financial advice? Yet, how often, for example, have we seen any of these so-called sages of the investment world recommend a convertible bond as a superior alternative to common stock? Either these "professionals" also don't understand the more sophisticated investment instruments, or they are afraid to lose subscriptions by writing "over the heads" of their readers. In either case, the public is the biggest loser.

Since truly worthwhile investment ideas are hard to find, where does one turn for superior advice or superior money management?

STOCK MARKET ALTERNATIVES—WHERE THE SMART MONEY IS

Students of Wall Street have said that if a new strategy were developed to beat the stock market it would be exploited by professional money managers so quickly that it would soon be rendered worthless.

Don't believe it!

Most money managers aren't receptive to new investment approaches involving nontraditional techniques. Rather, the vast majority simply cannot, or will not, employ the truly sophisticated tools available, e.g., convertibles, options, and short selling.

It would appear that most brokers or money managers would rather lose money via the traditional purchase of common stock than attempt to explain sophisticated strategies to their unsophisticated clients. From my own personal experience as a stockbroker during the 1974 bear market, certain clients were uncomfortable with a 10-percent paper loss in a strategy they did not fully comprehend but did not seem to be unduly alarmed that their common stock portfolios were down 50 percent, or more. And this is more often the rule rather than the exception. With the 1974 bear market driving so many investors away who may never return to the market, even many of the remaining investors don't seem to get upset when their stocks drop. Perhaps they are consoled by the fact that they're in good company with the Dow Jones Average or the institutional money managers.

Most of the strategies you are about to learn presently are not being employed by investment professionals. Yet, these approaches have given individual investors a source of extraordinary profits over the years together with the personal satisfaction of outperforming the market while the "pros" were not.

Do you know, for instance, that some very successful stock market investors *never* buy common stocks? It's true! Instead of stocks, they search out alternative opportunities that offer superior risk/reward advantages—advantages that might offer lower risk, greater profit potential, higher yield, or any combination of these objectives. These alternatives will be presented in this book along with examples of past opportunities for illustration. New strategies for today's market will also be presented and analyzed.

One of my favorite examples in recent times for illustrating the advantages inherent in selecting stock market alternatives has been Pan American World Airways—an actively traded stock that advanced from $2 per share in early 1975 to over $7 in 1976. How many buyers of this stock were even aware of the several Pan American convertible bonds available during this time period? For example, the Pan Am 7½s of 1998, convertible into 143 shares of common stock, traded at little or no premium over its conversion value. When Pan American stock was at $2, the bond was at 30; when the stock was at $3.50, the bond was at 50; and when the stock reached $7, the bond traded at 100. At all times the bond offered the same upside potential as the stock while providing a much higher yield than the nondividend-paying common—25 percent, for instance, at a price of 30! In addition, being a senior security, the bond provided *greater downside safety*. The common stock buyers simply overlooked an opportunity to increase their return on investment by 25 percent per year while assuming less risk! Situations such as this occur frequently. The smart money capitalizes on them. The conventional money ignores them.

Those who purchased Pan American common stock at $2 in early 1975 and still hold it today in early 1978 at a price of $5 are probably very pleased with their investment acumen. The stock has appreciated 150 percent during three difficult market years. But they could have done substantially better! Bond buyers, at a corresponding price of 30, have actually received 180 percent gain as the bond is now trading at 84. The market finally "discovered" that the bond was undervalued relative to the common and has assigned it a reasonable premium over its conversion value. In addition to the extra 30 percent capital gain, the bond provided 75 percent interest income for the three years—*a total advantage of 35 percent annually for a lower risk investment instrument.*

Perhaps you might consider Pan American to be too aggressive for your investment tastes under any circumstances. So let's look for a moment at the bluest of the blue chips to help illustrate my point. From 1972 to 1975, the short sale of AT&T warrants against AT&T's common stock nearly doubled one's investment while the total return for the higher risk strategy of owning the common stock unhedged was less than 50 percent for the three-year period.[1] How many investors never even considered the "speculative" short sale of AT&T warrants in 1972 but are now aggressively writing call options against their common stock portfolios? Yet, the AT&T warrants were grossly overpriced in 1972 while call options in today's market are fairly priced.

In the real world of investing, the stock market has offered a total annual return of about 8 to 9 percent over the very long term, and substantially less in recent years. No serious investor intent on beating the market can afford to overlook any of the many tools available for gaining an edge of even a few percentage points.

WHAT THIS BOOK IS ALL ABOUT

Since joining the investment community, I have written three books on advanced investment strategies prior to this one; the most recent, *How*

---

[1] Refer to chap. 12 of *How the Experts Beat the Market* for a complete analysis of the AT&T warrant hedge.

the Experts Beat the Market, was published in 1976. As the title implies, the strategies presented consistently outperformed the market over the years. However, successful strategies change continuously. Warrants, for example, have always been a popular tool of the sophisticated hedger. Undervalued warrants have been hedged by the short sale of common stock. Overpriced warrants like AT&T's have been sold short against common stock or convertibles. Tactics such as these were successfully employed by experienced hedgers who gained above average returns while limiting risk.

In *How the Experts Beat the Market,* I devoted four chapters to warrant hedging strategies. But as fewer companies have issued new warrants in recent years, outstanding hedging opportunities have become virtually nonexistent. Perhaps warrants may return to the investment arena at a later time, but for now we must look elsewhere for hedging opportunities. Accordingly, I have excluded warrant hedging strategies from this book.

Hedging with listed put and call options, on the other hand, is a viable tactic. Looking back a few years when listed call options first began trading on the Chicago Board Options Exchange, we see that options were highly overpriced. A successful hedging strategy at that time was to sell calls against their underlying common stocks. But as this strategy became more popular, option premiums plummeted and writing calls against common stock in today's market has become a *losing* strategy, as you will see in Chapter 6.

Furthermore, the demise of the warrant and the decline of call option premiums have caused a significant shifting of the strategies employed by experienced hedgers. Successful hedgers now place far more importance on selecting undervalued convertibles for the long side of their portfolios. Such a strategy permits the short sale of normally valued securities (call options or common stock) while still providing high profit potential at low risk. These traditional hedge strategies will be covered in detail in Chapters 7–9.

In *How the Experts Beat the Market,* I also introduced the Superhedge™ concept, the most exciting investment strategy I have ever used. The original Superhedge™ returned 60 percent during its first year (hard as it may be to believe) and 40 percent during its second year with less risk than a typical portfolio of the highest quality blue chip stocks. Although the original concept, SUPERHEDGE™ I, was ideally structured for the higher call option premiums prevailing during 1975–76, this strategy still offers superior investment opportunities for those investors having a bullish outlook on the stock market, as will be shown in Chapter 11.

Since SUPERHEDGE™ I was created in 1975, numerous alternatives have been developed. The Superhedge™ concept now offers investment opportunities for *all* investors whether their market outlook is bullish, bearish, or somewhere in between these extremes. These Superhedge™ alternatives have been introduced to a limited number of investors through *Advanced Investment Strategies*™,[2] an investment advisory service launched in July 1977.

The final chapters of this book will provide in-depth instructions on selecting and managing Superhedge™ portfolios suitable for bulls or bears, fundamentalists or technicians, or even "random walkers."

Before presenting these advanced hedging strategies, the next three chapters will cover straightforward alternatives to common stock investing. These alternatives will permit you to seek the full upside potential of the stock market while reducing your risk by half, or less. The alternatives are ideally suited for pension funds and other serious stock market investors who do not wish to employ hedging strategies to be presented later. Study this material carefully as it is intended to change completely your approach to investing in the market. It will also provide the necessary basics for the hedging strategies to be developed in later chapters. Chapter 4, in particular, presents a unique set of proven guidelines for superior performance at lower risk. Since the development and employment of these guidelines in late 1976, these rules have outscored the S&P 500 index by 30 percent over a 16-month period through April 1978 (brokerage commissions included). A complete track record will be shown.

---

[2] *Advanced Investment Strategies*™ is an investment advisory service published monthly by Thomas C. Noddings and Associates, Inc., 135 S. LaSalle St., Chicago, Ill. 60603.

2

UNDERVALUED CONVERTIBLES WILL OUTPERFORM THE MARKET

The experienced investor should *never buy* a share of common stock without first checking to see if there is a convertible security available that offers superior risk/reward characteristics. The random walker (or indexing proponent) should *never even consider owning common stock —there are far better alternatives!*

These statements are contrary to the preachings of most Wall Street "professionals"—even many of those who embrace the efficient market concept of investing. Nevertheless, the statements are known to be true by sophisticated investors around the country—investors who laugh at the simplistic advice provided by most brokerage firms and investment advisory services.

Undervalued convertibles of well-established companies should constitute the central holdings of your investment portfolio. These securities will also be used in the more advanced investment strategies to be presented later.

For purposes of this discussion, a convertible security is defined as either a convertible bond or a convertible preferred stock. Call options and warrants have related characteristics but are excluded from this narrow definition for ease of reference.

Any convertible may be compared with its underlying common stock by simple analytical measurements provided later in this chapter. Its potential upside reward and downside risk, relative to its stock, can be estimated with reasonable accuracy. After giving additional consideration to the yields of both securities, the convertible can be judged to be undervalued, normally valued, or overpriced relative to its common stock. The *undervalued* convertible should be purchased in lieu of the common, whereas the *overpriced* convertible should be sold or avoided

An undervalued convertible may offer the *same* upside profit opportunity as its common stock at *less* downside risk. Or it might offer *much* of the upside potential at *substantially less* risk. The convertible will also provide a yield advantage over its stock in terms of both its actual payout and the safety of that payout in most cases. If the convertible is a bond, its guaranteed redemption price provides an additional advantage.

Let us now turn to the real world of investing and evaluate typical convertibles as they are actually traded in the marketplace.

A NORMALLY PRICED CONVERTIBLE—CITICORP BONDS

In July 1975, Citicorp brought its first convertible to the market—a bond yielding 5¾ percent and exchangeable into 24.4 shares of common stock. It was quickly oversubscribed by institutional money managers, and Citicorp was happy to increase the size of its offering to $350 million in response to the enthusiastic reception. (It was the largest convertible bond issue on record at that time.)

A graphic analysis of the Citicorp bond in July 1975 is presented by Exhibit 2–1. A step-by-step evaluation of its risk/reward characteristic follows.

Conversion value. Each $1,000 bond was immediately convertible into 24.4 shares of common stock at the option of the bondholder. Its conversion value, as shown by the sloping solid line on Exhibit 2–1, is simply the market price of the stock multiplied by 24.4 shares. For example, the stock was trading at $36 per share when the bond was issued. The bond's conversion value at that time was:

$$24.4 \text{ shares} \times \$36 \text{ per share} = \$878$$

If the stock were to decline 25 percent to $27, the conversion value would be:

Exhibit 2–1
Citicorp 5¾ s–'00 convertible bond, July 1975 (issue size, $350 million; bond converts into 24.4 shares)

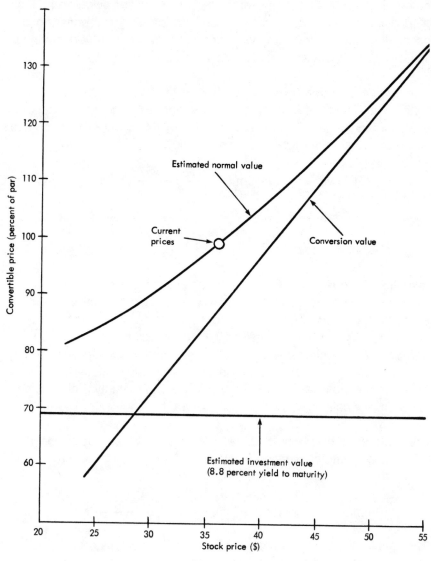

24.4 shares × $27 per share = $659

If the stock were to advance 25 percent to $45, the conversion value would be:

24.4 shares × $45 per share = $1,098

Since the conversion value is the bond's worth if the holder were to exchange it for common stock, any convertible must trade at or above its conversion value. Otherwise, professional arbitragers would profit by purchasing it below conversion value and simultaneously selling the underlying stock. Conversion value therefore provides a fixed but sloping "floor" under the market price of a convertible security.

Conversion premium.   A convertible's premium over its conversion value is an important tool for measuring worth. At an offering price of $1,000 when the underlying stock was trading at $36, the Citicorp bond's conversion premium was calculated as follows:

$$\text{Conversion premium} = \frac{\$1,000 - \$878}{\$878} = 14\%$$

Most new convertibles are issued at conversion premiums ranging from 10 to 15 percent. Most older convertibles will also trade in this premium range when they are near par.

Investment value.   The investment value of a convertible is its worth without its conversion privilege. This value is estimated by bond-rating services in the same way the services evaluate conventional nonconvertible bonds. The raters consider the inherent quality of the bond relative to prevailing interest rates for similar securities. As shown in Exhibit 2–1, the investment value for the high-quality Citicorp bond was estimated at $690 based on an 8.8 percent yield to maturity. This figure is shown as the solid horizontal line on the graph.

Premium over investment value.   For analytical purposes, the premium paid for the conversion privilege of the Citicorp bond may be expressed as a percentage over its investment value:

$$\text{Premium over investment value} = \frac{\$1,000 - \$690}{\$690} = 45\%$$

The smaller the premium over investment value, the less susceptible is the convertible to a price decline by its underlying stock since the investment value provides a price "floor" under the convertible. This floor may move up or down, however, with changing money market rates or with the changing fortunes of the company.

Yield advantage.   The Citicorp bonds, yielding 5¾ percent when issued at par, provided a yield advantage of 3.3 percent over the low dividend-paying common stock. Practically all new convertibles offer yield advantages. As time passes, however, the advantage may diminish as the common stock's dividend is increased.

Break-even time. Another analytical tool is the number of years it will take for the convertible's yield advantage to make up for its present premium over conversion value. The break-even time for the Citicorp bonds was:

$$\text{Break-even time} = \frac{14 \text{ percent conversion premium}}{3.3 \text{ percent yield advantage}} = 4.2 \text{ years}$$

A small break-even time (under five years) generally means that the convertible offers greater value than its common stock and should be purchased in lieu of the common. However, even convertibles having very long break-even times may be a superior alternative to their common stock if there is a possibility that the dividend may be reduced or eliminated on the stock. For the same reason, some convertibles are better even if their yields are below those of their stocks—Consolidated Edison's convertible preferred in 1974 was a good example. It was yielding about ½ percent less than its common and was trading close to its conversion value prior to the dividend omission on the common. The extra safety of the preferred's payout made it a far better investment than the common stock of Consolidated Edison.

Normal value curve. The normal value curve for the Citicorp bond, as shown in Exhibit 2–1, is an estimate of the future near-term price for the convertible at any stock price. This is the most important concept presented so far in this book. Taking into consideration all the variables previously discussed, the normal value curve may be calculated from complex mathematical formulas or approximated if you have experience and good judgment in this area.

The *upside* price estimates for any convertible are controlled by the conversion value, while *downside* price estimates are controlled by the floor provided by the investment value. Since the conversion value is fixed, upside estimates may be made with exceptional accuracy. Downside estimates, however, are subject to uncertainties because the investment value may move up or down with changing money market rates independent of the price action of the underlying common stock—or the market may ignore theoretical investment values during emotional sell-offs.

Risk/reward analysis. By using the normal value curve from Exhibit 2–1, we may now make a complete comparison of Citicorp's convertible bond with its underlying common stock in July 1975. Assuming that the common stock would remain unchanged, or advance or decline by either 25 or 50 percent during the following 12 months, a risk/reward analysis of both securities may be made as shown in the accompanying table.

As conclusively demonstrated by this risk/reward analysis, the normally valued Citicorp convertible bond was a superior alternative to its common stock. Its downside risk was only one third of the common while it provided more than three fourths of the upside potential.

	Assumed stock price change (next 12 months)				
	−50%	*−25%*	*0%*	*+25%*	*+50%*
Stock price	18	27	36	45	54
Estimated bond price	78	87	100	116	133
Stock gain or loss	−50%	−25%	0%	+ 25%	+ 50%
Plus dividends	+ 2	+ 2	+ 2	+ 2	+ 2
Net gain or loss	−48%	−23%	+ 2%	+ 27%	+ 52%
Convertible gain or loss	−22%	−13%	0%	+ 16%	+ 33%
Plus interest	+ 6	+ 6	+ 6	+ 6	+ 6
Net gain or loss	−16%	− 7%	+ 6%	+ 22%	+ 39%

RULE NO. 1. Never buy a share of common stock without first checking to see if there is a convertible having superior risk/reward characteristics. Even normally priced convertibles may offer advantages over their underlying common stocks.

AN UNDERVALUED CONVERTIBLE—CHASE MANHATTAN BONDS

While the institutional money managers throughout the country were scrambling to get their share of the record-size Citicorp issue, the convertible bonds of Citicorp's sister bank, Chase Manhattan, were avoided by the investment community. In July 1975 both of these high-quality bank stocks were trading at about $36, and both declined to below $30 during the next few months. The Chase Manhattan bonds were undervalued throughout this period but attracted little buying interest.

Exhibit 2–2 provides a graphic analysis of the Chase Manhattan convertibles in November 1975, similar to the previous analysis for Citicorp.

Exhibit 2–2
Chase Manhattan 4⅞s–'93 convertible bond, November 1975 (issue size, $150 million; bond converts into 18.18 shares)

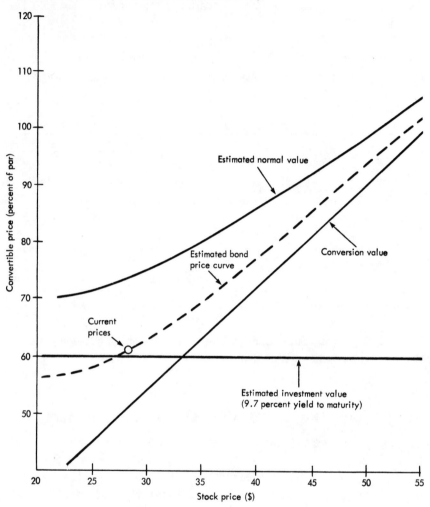

Strange as it seems, the Chase Bonds were actually trading within 2 percent of their estimated investment value while at only a modest 20-percent premium above conversion value. They were clearly a far better buy than their underlying common stock.

Historical experience shows that an undervalued convertible will tend to remain undervalued for long periods of time. The *estimated bond price curve* of Exhibit 2–2 reflects this experience and assumes that the Chase bonds will be no exception. In spite of this conservative assumption, they offered nearly three fourths the upside potential of the common at little or no downside risk. And if they ever returned to their normal value curve, greater relative advantage than indicated would be achieved.

Risk/reward analysis.   A risk/reward analysis for the Chase Manhattan securities, similar to the previous analysis for Citicorp, is shown in the accompanying table.

	Assumed stock price change (next 12 months)				
	−50%	*−25%*	*0%*	*+25%*	*+50%*
Stock price	14	21	28	35	42
Estimated bond price	55	57	61	70	81
Stock gain or loss	−50%	−25%	0%	+25%	+50%
Plus dividends	+ 8	+ 8	+ 8	+ 8	+ 8
Net gain or loss	−42%	−17%	+ 8%	+33%	+58%
Convertible gain or loss	−10%	− 6%	0%	+15%	+33%
Plus interest	+ 8	+ 8	+ 8	+ 8	+ 8
Net gain or loss	− 2%	+ 2%	+ 8%	+23%	+41%

RULE NO. 2.   Undervalued convertibles offer substantial advantages over their underlying common stocks and should always be purchased in lieu of the common.

THE CITICORP AND CHASE MANHATTAN BONDS IN 1978

The selection of the Citicorp and Chase Manhattan bonds, to illustrate important features, was made in 1975 for *How the Experts Beat the Market.* The material presented in this chapter was taken directly from that book without modification. The actual market movement of these securities has been surprising. The once popular Citicorp common stock has plunged nearly 50 percent from $36 down to $19 per share while their bonds have declined 25 percent from par down to 75—a somewhat greater decline for the bonds than was expected, but still *much less* than that of the stock.

Chase Manhattan stock on the other hand is unchanged at $28, but the bonds have actually advanced more than 20 percent from 61 to 74. Chase bonds are now trading closer to their estimated normal value curve shown in Exhibit 2–2.

BUYING CONVERTIBLES ON MARGIN

The ability to purchase securities on margin gives the individual investor greater flexibility than what most professional money managers have. For example, suppose that both an individual and a pension fund portfolio manager concluded that the common stock of Chase Manhattan was grossly oversold in November 1975 at $28 per share. They were both sure the stock would advance 50 percent within the next 12 months. The pension fund manager, pressured by increasing demand for better performance, might reject the convertible bond because it offered less upside potential than the common stock (41 percent versus 58 percent). The individual, however, should not even consider the common stock but instead should purchase the convertible bonds on margin. The risk/reward postures for the two investors would be as shown in the table.

	Assumed stock price change		
	−50%	*0%*	*+50%*
Common stock purchased for cash	−42	+8	+58
Bonds purchased on 50 percent margin (assuming margin interest at 8 percent)	−12	+8	+74

RULE NO. 3.   The purchase of an undervalued convertible on margin may be a prudent alternative to the cash purchase of its underlying common stock.

Again, history has shown that the margined purchase of the Chase Manhattan bonds would have provided a capital gain of over 40 percent by March 1978 (plus 8 percent annual cash flow) while the stock remained unchanged.

UNDERVALUED CONVERTIBLES FOR AGGRESSIVE INVESTORS

The most undervalued convertible securities are frequently related to stocks that do not have an institutional following. Investors and speculators alike often buy and sell these stocks unaware that a convertible exists; thus price inefficiencies between the related securities occur quite often as the convertibles are overlooked by the marketplace.

Exhibits 2–3 and 2–4 illustrate two grossly undervalued convertible bonds available to aggressive investors during 1975—LTV and Pan

Exhibit 2–3
**LTV 7½ s–'77 convertible bond, January 1975 (issue size, $36 million; bond
converts into 95.24 shares)**

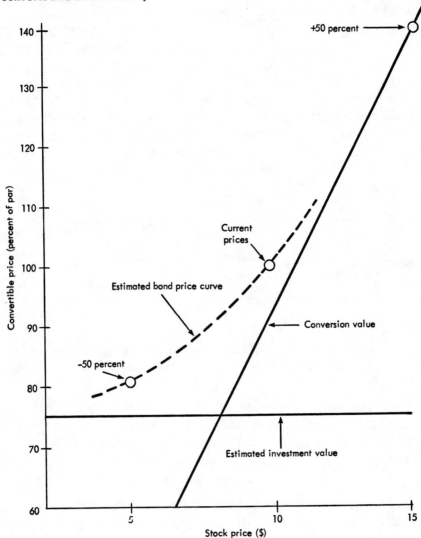

Exhibit 2–4
Pan American 7½ s–'98 convertible bond, October 1975 (issue size, $75 million; bond converts into 142.86 shares)

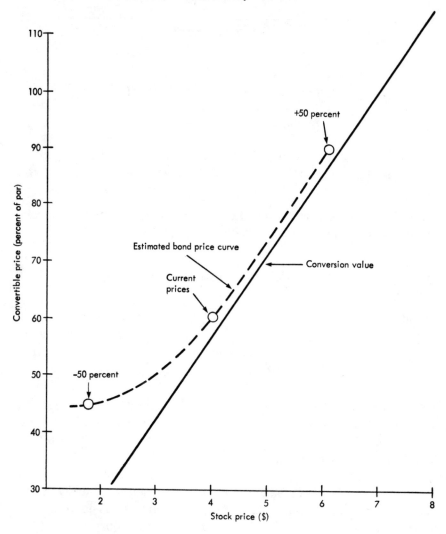

American. Risk/reward estimates, assuming a 12-month position, were as shown in this table.

	Assumed stock price change		
	−50%	*0%*	*+50%*
Stock gain or loss	−50	0	+50
Gain or loss for convertibles			
LTV	−13	+ 7	+50
Pan American	−12	+13	+60

Anyone who purchased the common stock of LTV or Pan American made a serious investment error. The bonds *were certain* to provide as much (or more) upside potential at substantially less downside risk.

RULE NO. 4.   Grossly undervalued convertibles are often found on stocks that do not have an institutional following.

WHAT HAPPENED TO THE LTV AND PAN AMERICAN BONDS?

As with Citicorp and Chase Manhattan, the material presented in this chapter for LTV and Pan American convertible bonds was taken directly from *How the Experts Beat the Market* without change. How did each of these aggressive convertibles fare?

The LTV bonds advanced to near 190 as LTV's common stock reached a recovery high of $19¾ later in 1975. The bonds provided the upside appreciation of LTV common stock while their 1977 maturity date protected the investor from loss.

The Pan American bonds also offered a profit-taking opportunity as the common advanced to near $8 in 1976; and the bonds to over 110. Later, as the stock pulled back, the market began to appreciate that the bonds were grossly undervalued and their price stayed above the estimated bond price curve of Exhibit 2–4 during the decline. At a stock price of $5 in early 1978 (a 25-percent gain from $4 per share in October 1975) the bonds were trading at 84 or a 40-percent advance from 60. Not only did bond holders of Pan Am receive greater capital appreciation; they also earned 13 percent annual interest while the stockholders received nothing. This again demonstrates that bonds are capable of providing as much upside potential as stock (in this case substantially more) at significantly less downside risk.

PLACING ORDERS FOR CONVERTIBLE BONDS

The following guidelines should be followed carefully when placing buy or sell orders for convertible bonds.

Select bonds that are actively traded whenever possible—they will normally be listed on the New York Stock Exchange and have a large issue outstanding.

Monitor both the bond and its underlying stock prices prior to entering orders—a good "feel" for their related prices will save you money, whether buying or selling, by permitting you to execute orders at favorable prices. Or, give this monitoring responsibility to your broker.

Place orders through a brokerage firm that has skills in executing orders in both the listed and over-the-counter bond markets—many listed bonds are more actively traded in the over-the-counter mar-market than on the floor of the exchange.

Work with a stockbroker who has special training in evaluating convertibles and in executing orders—the broker's knowledge and skills are much more critical to your investment success in this area than in conventional buying or selling of common stocks.

RULE NO. 5.   By working with a stockbroker skilled in the use of convertible securities, you will gain additional profits.

CONVERTIBLE BONDS VERSUS CONVERTIBLE PREFERREDS

Since convertible bonds and convertible preferreds have many similar characteristics, both may be evaluated on such factors as conversion value, investment value, and yield advantage. Yet, there are some significant differences which may influence investment strategy.

Claim on assets.   Since bondholder claims to a company's assets are senior to those of preferred stockholders, bonds are inherently safer. This distinction may be of little consequence if the company is financially sound. For a speculative company, however, it may be of major importance.

Continuity of payments.   During adverse times, a company will suspend dividends on its preferred stock before discontinuing bond interest payments—the failure of a company to meet bond interest obligations places it in default, the first step toward bankruptcy. Even though the dividends paid on preferred stock are usually cumulative (arrearages must be made up before dividends are paid to common shareholders), holders of preferred stock may have a long wait before receiving the dividends, once suspended. Eventually, they may even have to accept some sort of exchange offer from the company and may, therefore, never see the dividend arrearages paid.

Tax consequences. Dividends paid on preferred stocks (or common stocks) possess unique tax advantages over interest received on bonds. Bond interest is fully taxable as ordinary income, whereas the first $100 of annual dividends is excluded on individual tax returns ($200 on joint returns). The tax advantage to corporations is even greater because they are permitted to exclude 85 percent of the dividends received on most preferreds (and common stocks). These tax benefits to corporations have historically kept the yields of preferreds close to bonds despite the greater safety of the bond.

Maturity date. Since bonds have a fixed maturity date, they must ultimately be redeemed by the company at par value. An approaching maturity date provides additional protection against broad price swings caused by interest rate changes. It may also protect the convertible bond against a serious price decline by the common stock without limiting its upside potential. Preferred stocks, which seldom have a maturity date, are more sensitive to changing market conditions.

RULE NO. 6. **All other factors being equal, a convertible bond is usually better than a convertible preferred for the individual investor.**

SPECIAL CONVERTIBLES

Our discussion up to now has covered conventional types of convertible bonds and preferreds—those immediately exchangeable into a fixed number of common stock shares. These represent by far the largest part of the convertible securities market. Yet, there are several types of special convertibles that can offer unusual risk/reward opportunities, and all sophisticated investors should be familiar with them.

Plus cash convertible. This is a convertible security that requires an additional cash payment upon conversion. Since the cash payment is constant regardless of the common stock's market price, the conversion value changes faster than the price of the underlying common stock. This type of special convertible may be of interest to the investor seeking greater leverage than that offered by conventional convertibles.

Fabricated convertible. This special convertible is a combination of warrants plus straight bonds that may be used at par value (usually $1,000) in lieu of the cash exercise price when exercising the warrants. To determine the number of warrants to be purchased with each straight bond, simply divide the par value of the bond by the total exercise price of the warrant. The combination results in risk/reward characteristics similar to conventional convertibles but provides greater flexibility as the bonds and warrants are purchased or sold separately.

Unit convertible. This is a convertible issue that, instead of being exchangeable into only common stock, is instead convertible into a "unit" —a package of one or more securities that may not even include the common. The evaluation of a unit convertible requires additional sophistication but can be potentially more rewarding since the marketplace may have extra difficulty in assigning a normal value.

Delayed convertible. The most exciting, and potentially rewarding, special convertibles are bonds or preferred stocks having delayed conversion features and selling at a discount below their future conversion value. These generally fall into either of two categories:

A convertible with fixed conversion terms that specify the number of shares of common stock to be received upon conversion beginning at a specified future date. Price action of the convertible will be related to that of the common stock.

A convertible that will convert into common stock beginning on a specified date based upon a formula relating to the future price of the common. Depending on the specific terms, the convertible's price action prior to the date it becomes convertible may or may not be related to that of its common stock.

RULE NO. 7. Special convertibles may offer unusually attractive risk/reward opportunities to the sophisticated investor.

UNUSUAL PLUSES AND MINUSES

The complex field of convertible securities offers unusual opportunities to the sophisticated investor—and hidden traps to the unwary.

Short-term convertible bonds. A convertible bond nearing its maturity date may resist decline if its common stock drops while still offering upside potential if the stock advances.

Preferreds in arrears.   This situation offers potentially high profits to the aggressive investor if the previously omitted dividends are cumulative and the company is a turnaround candidate.

Tender offers for discounted bonds.   In an effort to improve its balance sheet, a company may make a cash tender or exchange offer for its discounted bonds. The value offered is usually well above the current market price of the bond to assure a favorable response.

Changes in terms.   Some convertibles have fixed schedules for changing their conversion terms at future specified dates. These changes are usually downward and will therefore reduce the value of the convertible.

Expiration of conversion privileges.   The conversion privilege of some convertibles may terminate well before the maturity date. At that time, the convertible's price will immediately drop to its investment value.

Call provisions.   Be extra careful of paying a conversion premium if the convertible is subject to call at a price below its current market value. If called, the convertible will immediately drop to its conversion value. In addition, the interest accrued on a bond since its last interest payment date may be lost.

Mergers and tender offers for the common stock.   These events may have either positive or negative impact on the market value of a convertible, depending on the specific terms of the package offered to the common stockholders and the convertible's premium over conversion value.

Antidilution provisions.   Convertibles are generally protected against stock splits, stock dividends, etc. However, there have been instances where a company has spun off a subsidiary to holders of its common stock without adjusting the conversion terms of its convertibles. You will probably be unable to protect yourself against such deceitful tactics used by some corporate officials.

RULE NO. 8.   The sophisticated investor will profit from a keen awareness of the potential opportunities and hidden traps in the area of convertible securities.

3

BUYING THE STOCK MARKET AT A DISCOUNT

Closed-end funds as a group represent some of the most overlooked investment opportunities in today's stock market. They are ideally suited for the smaller pension funds and individual investors who desire both market diversification and professional portfolio management. Larger investors may also employ these funds in certain advanced hedging strategies, as will be covered in later chapters.

Closed-end funds are attractive because most sell at large discounts from their net asset values. Many attempts have been made to explain why the funds generally trade at discounts, but the only plausible answer that I can accept is that no one has a real incentive to sell them. Fund managers have no reason to spend advertising dollars promoting this type of investment since the fund's assets, and hence the related management fees, are fixed. And brokers prefer to sell mutual funds which provide a much higher sales commission than closed-end funds. The latter generate only the normal commission attached to listed stocks.

Two types of closed-end funds command the interest of investors skilled in the areas of convertibles and hedging. They are: the convertible funds and the capital shares of the dual-purpose funds.

THE CONVERTIBLE FUNDS

The closed-end convertible funds offer the opportunity for the smaller investor to attain diversification while gaining an edge on the stock

Exhibit 3–1

Fund	Exchange	Symbol	Assets (in $ million)	New asset value per share	Price	Discount	Current dividend	Current yield
American General Convertible Securities	NYSE	AGS	68.4	$22.03	$16⅞	−23.4%	$1.32	7.8%
Bancroft Convertible Fund	ASE	BCV	46.1	22.41	18⅛	−19.1	1.11	6.1
Castle Convertible Fund	ASE	CVF	24.6	24.73	20	−19.1	1.68	8.4
Chase Convertible Fund	NYSE	CFB	62.8	11.39	9⅛	−19.9	0.60	6.6

Note: All statistics as of December 30, 1977.

market. The four funds currently existing are all publicly traded. Exhibit 3–1 will acquaint you with their names and basic characteristics.

The stated objective of each of these funds is to invest at least 80 percent of their assets in convertible bonds and preferreds. Like all closed-end and mutual (open-end) funds, these funds are regulated investment companies. This means that they are not taxed on their investment income as long as at least 90 percent of their income flows to the shareholders. Capital gains (if any) are distributed annually. All of these funds may employ leverage (through bank borrowing against portfolio holdings), although none are doing so at the present time.

The investment philosophy of the funds seems to follow my own thinking on convertibles; namely, a portfolio of convertibles will participate in market advances with less participation in market declines. Seeking the higher yields available on convertibles is another commonly stated goal. An evaluation of the above table shows that each of the funds offers higher current yields than the popular stock market indices—a fact ignored by most brokers and financial advisers.

Each of these funds is authorized to hold nonconvertible securities. When common stocks, warrants, and nonconvertible debt instruments are obtained through conversions or tender offers, these securities may be held for indefinite periods of time as well. The funds may also shift to heavier cash and short-term note positions when their managers deem it advisable. Exhibit 3–2 shows an analysis of the current holdings of the funds. Obviously, there is a divergence between each fund's commitment to investing in convertibles.

Exhibit 3–2

	Convertibles	Other investments		
		Common stocks	Nonconvertible bonds	Cash and notes
American General	66.0%	10.5%	21.0%	2.5%
Bancroft	91.5	7.0	—	1.5
Castle	83.4	14.2	—	2.4
Chase	73.8	3.5	4.2	18.5

The convertible funds have outperformed the market since their inception a few years ago, as measured from net asset value and assuming reinvestment of dividends. Exhibit 3–3 shows their performance over the four-year period beginning September 1973 and compares it with the

Exhibit 3–3
Convertible funds performance records

	End September 1976–77	End September 1975–77	End September 1974–77	End September 1973–77
American General	+10.9	+50.4	+ 95.0	+51.7
Bancroft	+ 9.3	+42.8	+ 89.6	+50.0
Castle	+16.0	+62.7	+115.2	+63.5
Chase	+ 8.1	+42.8	+ 79.2	+35.7
Average	+11.1	+49.7	+ 94.8	+50.2
S&P 500	− 4.3	+24.7	+ 72.2	+ 5.1

Source: Davis-Dinsmore Management Company.

total return of the S&P 500 for the same period. It's interesting to note that not only did the funds post gains during the past reporting year (1976–77), a year in which the S&P 500 declined, but also that they have *outperformed rising markets* as well. From the end of the bear market in 1974, the funds have gained an average of 94.8 percent compared with the S&P 500 at 72.2 percent. Yet brokers and financial advisers continue to look the other way.

The point is simply this: Investors in convertibles can expect to participate in rising markets and yet have the cushion they want and need to protect them in falling markets. Based on past performance, the four funds have demonstrated their ability to achieve this goal time and again!

Is the discount from net asset value a major advantage? Probably not, but neither is it a disadvantage. Unlike the dual-purpose funds to be discussed shortly, the convertible funds have no terminal date to insure eventual redemption at net asset value. Because of the discount dividends and future performance are favorably leveraged, but the significant edge to be gained is the result of the employment of carefully selected convertible securities in their portfolios.

In conclusion, the closed-end convertible funds are well suited for small investment accounts (such as Keogh and IRA plans) where the advantages of convertible investing are important but where diversification may be a problem.

THE DUAL-PURPOSE FUNDS

Dual-purpose funds can be used by both conservative and aggressive investors to gain substantial advantages over conventional forms of investing. More income can be obtained than from corporate bonds, or greater capital appreciation can be sought at less risk than from the typical common stock portfolio.

Dual-purpose funds are ideal tools for the individual investor. It is unfortunate that most investors don't understand them, but if everyone did, the advantages offered by these unique investments would no longer exist. What are the advantages? How are they measured? These questions will be answered, but first let us understand the subject at hand.

The dual-purpose funds are closed-end investment companies with portfolios similar to those of other professionally managed funds. However, as the term "dual-purpose" implies, fund ownership is divided equally into two classes of securities—income shares and capital shares. The *income* shares receive all the dividends and interest earned on the underlying portfolio while the *capital* shares get all the capital gains, or losses. Therefore, an investor can have $2 working toward his particular goal for each $1 that he invests. "Leveraged fund" is a term commonly used to describe this feature.

Dual-purpose funds also differ from other closed-end funds in another most important, but overlooked, area. Each dual-purpose fund has a specified *terminal date* when there will be a final accounting to both the income and the capital shareholders. The funds will either liquidate or become open-end investment companies (mutual funds) as desired by the shareholders. The income shares will be redeemed at fixed prices, and the remaining assets will go to the capital shareholders. Payment will be in cash or in equivalent value of shares of the ongoing mutual fund (which may be redeemed at net asset value).

Before the terminal date, neither class of shares can be redeemed, and all are traded in the marketplace. Like other closed-end funds, their market prices may reflect either a discount or a premium relative to their net assets, and they have generally sold at discounts since their inception in 1967. This discount is the most important advantage offered by the dual-purpose funds and is the reason they are, for the present, such a unique and clearly superior investment. This advantage is especially attractive because unlike other funds, the terminal dates *provide fixed points in time when they must sell at their net asset values!* In other words, the discount *must disappear.*

At the present time, the seven dual-purpose funds shown in Exhibit 3–4 offer superior alternatives to conventional investments for income or capital appreciation or a combination of both objectives.

Exhibit 3–4

Funds	Investment adviser	Total assets (in $ million)
American DualVest Fund	Weiss, Peck & Greer	$ 37
Gemini Fund	Wellington Management	62
Hemisphere Fund	CNA Management Corp.	17
Income and Capital Shares	Phoenix Investment Council of Boston	28
Leverage Fund of Boston	Vance, Sanders & Co.	61
Putnam Duofund	The Putnam Management	29
Scudder Duo-Vest	Scudder, Stevens & Clark	102

The purchase of an equal number of income and capital shares of any of these dual-purpose funds would be comparable to investing in typical closed-end or mutual funds. However, each income and capital share should be evaluated separately to determine its individual merits. Procedures for studying these securities will be provided, but first we will trace the history of one of the funds to develop a better understanding of the advantages and related risks for these unusual securities.

GEMINI FUND

Gemini Fund began operations in March 1967, and except for modest cash reserves from time to time, its portfolio has been fully invested in a broadly diversified list of common stocks. Approximately 1.7 million shares of both income and capital securities were issued. Each had a starting new asset value of $11 per share (the shares were actually sold to the public above their net asset values since a sales charge was added.)

The total assets of the fund appreciated steadily through 1972, at which time they reached $55 million, compared to the starting value of $37 million. The 1973–74 bear market reduced net assets to $30 million, and they then rebounded to $62 million at the end of 1977. Overall, Gemini performed very satisfactorily during this difficult ten-year market period when most stock market portfolios declined in value. In fact, Gemini Fund was the standout performer of the dual-purpose fund group.

The purchasers of *income* shares in 1967 were promised a minimum annual dividend of $0.56 per share plus the possibility of future increases if the dividends received from the fund's portfolio increased. They were also guaranteed an $11 redemption value on December 31, 1984, unless the total assets of the fund were to shrink below $18.5 million by that date (1.7 million shares × $11 per share). The income shareholders have not been disappointed. In fact, the annual dividends paid on their shares have grown to $1.55—or a yield of 14 percent on the original $11 investment. The shares have traded as high as $17; well above their $11 redemption value despite the high interest rate levels prevailing in the long-term money markets.

Contrary to the investment objectives of the income shareholders, the buyers of *capital* shares in 1967 were seeking an aggressive way to participate in an advancing stock market. Had stocks continued to rise as they did during previous years, the capital shares would have advanced about twice as fast because of their inherent leverage. For example, if the total net assets of Gemini Fund had doubled to $74 million, the capital shares net asset value would have tripled to $33 per share—an appreciation of 200 percent. The capital shareholders would have also benefited from the lower tax rate applicable to capital gains. On the downside, however, the net asset value of the capital shares would have declined twice as fast as the total assets of the fund. Trading at $11 per share in 1967, the capital shares were simply a leveraged investment on the market—twice the upside potential but also twice the downside risk. The purchase of the capital shares provided an investment posture similar to buying conventional common stocks on 50 percent margin.

The discount for Gemini's capital shares, as 1978 began, offered an outstanding investment opportunity. On December 31, 1984, the capital shares *must* trade at their net asset value whether the public is an active participant in the stock market or not. At about $19 per share, the capital shares promised to advance more than twice as fast as the net assets of the fund over the next seven years. On the downside, their risk was cushioned by the large discount from net asset value.

Anyone interested in taking a long-term investment posture in the stock market should seriously consider Gemini's securities—or those of other dual-purpose funds—instead of building his own stock portfolio. The advantages are overwhelming! They include, as an alternative to a common stock portfolio:

Built-in diversification.

Professional money management.

One decision investing.

As a unique investment vehicle, the funds also offer:

Discount investing.

Leverage on your dollar (better than 2 for 1), offering the potential for outperforming an up market by a wide margin.

Let us now examine each of the income and capital shares of the seven funds as they existed on December 30, 1977, to determine which offered the best risk/reward characteristics.

THE DUAL-PURPOSE FUND INCOME SHARES

The income shares of the dual-purpose funds may be considered as alternate investments to corporate bonds or other income securities, or they may be combined with capital shares for an alternative to ordinary mutual funds or conventional common stock portfolios. Like bonds, their current yield and yield to maturity may be calculated. Exhibit 3–5 pro-

Exhibit 3–5
The income shares (December 30, 1977, values)

	Market prices	Redemption		Estimated dividend*	Current yield*	Yield to maturity*
		Price	Date			
American DualVest Fund	$14.25	$15.00	6/29/79	$0.87	6.1%	9.5%
Gemini Fund	16.625	11.00	12/31/84	1.55	9.3	5.4
Hemisphere Fund	8.50	11.44	6/30/85	0.64	7.5	10.7
Income and Capital Shares	10.625	10.00	3/31/82	0.88	8.3	7.0
Leverage Fund of Boston	14.25	13.72	1/03/82	1.09	7.6	6.8
Putnam Duofund	17.00	19.75	1/03/83	1.56	9.2	11.7
Scudder Duo-Vest	9.125	9.15	3/31/82	0.72	7.8	7.8

* Current yield and yield to maturity were based on dividends paid in 1977. No adjustments were made for possible dividend increases or decreases in future years.

vides relevant information at 1977 year-end prices. As shown in Exhibit 3–5, some of the shares offered higher returns than most corporate bonds having similar maturity dates.

As with the purchase of bonds, an investor considering these income shares should evaluate the quality of the underlying assets in the fund's portfolio and the amount of total assets relative to the redemption price (asset coverage). Exhibit 3–6 summarizes the essential information at 1977 year-end prices, but the fund's most recent quarterly report should be consulted also for complete and current data. As shown in Exhibit 3–6, most of the income shares were well protected by excess assets. The obvious exception was Hemisphere Fund since its asset coverage was only nominal. However, much of Hemisphere's assets were invested in short-term money market instruments or bonds and the balance in high-quality common stocks. Of course, portfolio shifts by the funds to more aggressive investments would expose their income shares to greater risk than indicated—or a shift to cash or bonds would increase safety.

Exhibit 3–6
The income shares (December 30, 1977, portfolio analysis)

	Redemption price	Current total assets*	Asset coverage	Portfolio makeup Cash and bonds†	Stocks‡
American DualVest Fund	$15.00	$23.22§	155%	21%	79%
Gemini Fund	11.00	37.00	336	0	100
Hemisphere Fund	11.44	12.08	106	46	54
Income and Capital Shares	10.00	18.63§	186	33	67
Leverage Fund of Boston	13.72	30.25	220	19	81
Putnam Duofund‖	19.75	38.33§	194	5	95
Scudder Duo-Vest	9.15	18.45	202	13	87

* Total assets equal income share redemption price plus capital share net asset value except as indicated §.

† Includes short-term money market instruments plus corporate or government bonds.

‡ Includes common stocks and convertible securities.

§ Current asset value for income share is less than redemption price—difference made up by terminal date by transfer of funds from capital shares to income shares:

American DualVest $14.75
Income and Capital Shares 9.81
Putnam Duofund 19.15

‖ Two capital shares for each income share.

During the 1973–74 bear market, the total assets of some of the funds declined to levels where the full redemption value of their income shares was threatened. This caused their portfolio managers to adopt defensive investment postures by switching some of their common stocks into cash or conservative income situations. For example, Hemisphere Fund was 98 percent in cash and bonds at the end of 1974. Assuming the same defensive money management strategy in the future, it seems reasonable to expect that the full redemption values will be received at terminal dates even if the stock market declines in interim years.

At 1977 year-end price levels, the income share group offered exceptional alternatives to corporate bonds or other conservative income-type
investments. Maturity dates from as short as 1½ years (American Dual-
Vest) to as long as 7½ years (Hemisphere Fund) provide additional flexibility for investment planning.

THE DUAL-PURPOSE FUND CAPITAL SHARES

My investment career has been devoted to the search for undervalued
or overpriced securities in the areas of convertibles, warrants, options,
and other special situations. This research has exposed many outstanding investment opportunities, but few compare with the dual-purpose
fund capital shares as they existed in January 1978. They were *grossly
undervalued* relative to the underlying assets in their portfolios. This unusual situation was caused by the lack of interest by the investment public. The institutions aggressively purchased the stocks held by the dual-
purpose funds, but there was little public activity to keep the shares of
the funds in line with their inherent values. And, for *strange* reasons, institutions *do not buy the securities of other professionally managed
funds*—even at huge discounts. Since these securities will probably remain undervalued for some time in the future in today's institutionally
dominated market, you should learn how to evaluate the risk/reward
characteristics of these capital shares. The following material should be
carefully studied—*then restudied.*

The capital shares of the dual-purpose funds are essentially long-term
call options (or warrants) on the underlying securities held by the funds.
At their terminal dates, they will be worth the total value of the funds'
portfolios less the fixed redemption prices paid to the income shareholders. Their potential upside appreciation and downside risk are directly
related to their current discounts below net asset values, their inherent
leverage, future stock market trends, and the investment skills of the
funds' managers.

The net asset value of a capital share is equal to the total assets of the
fund less the book value of its related income shares. This information
is reported weekly in *The Wall Street Journal* and other financial publications as shown in Exhibit 3–7. As useful as this published information
may seem, it does not provide the essential tools for measuring the true
worth of these securities. It provides no information on their inherent
leverage relative to the underlying equity-type investments in the fund—
information needed for evaluating their risk/reward characteristics.

Exhibit 3–7
The capital shares (December 30, 1977, values as reported weekly in financial publications)

	Market price	Net asset value	Premium or discount
American DualVest Fund	$ 7.25	$ 8.47	−14%
Gemini Fund	19.00	26.00	−27
Hemisphere Fund	1.25	0.64	+95
Income and Capital Shares	6.00	8.82	−32
Leverage Fund of Boston	11.875	16.53	−28
Putnam Duofund	6.375	9.59	−34
Scudder Duo-Vest	6.875	9.30	−26

Exhibits 3–8 and 3–9 bridge this information gap. As shown in Exhibit 3–8, we will assume the equity securities held in each of the funds' portfolios will simply advance or decline by the same amount as the overall stock market in future years. The net asset value at terminal date for each of the capital shares may then be estimated as shown. The dollar figures are converted to percentage advances or declines as shown in Exhibit 3–9.

Exhibit 3–8
The capital shares (estimated values at terminal dates)

		Estimated capital share value at terminal date,* assuming that equity portion of portfolio changes by:				
	Market price	−50%	−25%	0%	+50%	+100%
American DualVest Fund	$ 7.25	$ 0	$ 3.63	$ 8.22	$17.39	$26.56
Gemini Fund	19.00	7.50	16.75	26.00	44.50	63.00
Hemisphere Fund	1.25	0	0	0.64	3.90	7.16
Income and Capital Shares	6.00	2.39	5.51	8.63	14.87	21.11
Leverage Fund of Boston	11.875	4.28	10.40	16.53	28.78	41.03
Putnam Duofund†	6.375	0.18	4.74	9.29	18.40	27.50
Scudder Duo-Vest	6.875	1.27	5.29	9.30	17.33	25.35

* Estimated capital share value = current total assets (CTA), from Exhibit 3–6, plus or minus CTA X percent market change X percent of portfolio in equity investments, minus income share redemption value.

† Two capital shares for each income share.

Finally, risk/reward ratios may be computed for measuring the current attractiveness of each capital share relative to the overall stock market. I have selected a stock market advance of 50 percent versus a decline of 25 percent to calculate the risk/reward ratios, but other numbers may also be used if you desire. Since by definition the risk/reward ratio for

Exhibit 3–9
The capital shares (risk/reward analysis)

		Change in capital share value at terminal date, assuming that equity portion of portfolio changes by:				Risk/ reward ratio*
	−50%	*−25%*	*−0%*	*+50%*	*+100%*	
American DualVest Fund	−100%	− 50%	+13%	+140%	+266%	1.4
Gemini Fund	− 61	− 12	+37	+134	+232	5.6
Hemisphere Fund	−100	−100	−49	+212	+473	1.1
Income and Capital Shares	− 60	− 8	+44	+148	+252	9.3
Leverage Fund of Boston	− 64	− 12	+39	+142	+245	5.9
Putnam Duofund	− 97	− 26	+46	+188	+331	3.6
Scudder Duo-Vest	− 82	− 23	+35	+152	+268	3.3

$$* \text{ Risk/reward ratio} = \frac{25 \text{ percent market decline}}{\text{Percent capital share decline}} \times \frac{\text{Percent capital share advance}}{50 \text{ percent market advance}}$$

the "market" is 1.0, most of the dual-purpose fund capital shares offered substantial advantages.

CONCLUSIONS

The income shares and the capital shares of the dual-purpose funds have been overlooked by the investment public in the institutionally dominated stock market we have witnessed in recent times. Both presently offer outstanding values and can be used by the sophisticated investor in a variety of ways to improve investment performance. Here are a few strategies for your consideration.

1. Selected income shares offer greater current yield or yield-to-maturity than conventional income-type investments of comparable quality.

2. Selected capital shares provide an aggressive investment approach for achieving exceptional long-term capital appreciation—assuming a rising stock market in future years.

3. A combination of selected income shares and capital shares in different funds provides a superior alternative to conventional portfolios of common stock—an equal dollar amount invested in each offers greater upside potential at less downside risk. Investors in high-tax brackets should consider combining capital shares with tax-exempt bonds as a superior after-tax alternative to the stock market.

A 28-MONTH "TRACK RECORD"

During the weekend seminar on advanced investment strategies held in Chicago in November 1975, I strongly urged those attending to employ the capital shares of the dual-purpose funds as a superior buy and hold alternative to their conventional common stock portfolios. Again, in my book, *How the Experts Beat the Market,* I described the dual-purpose funds as *the most undervalued securities in the market* and provided statistical data as of December 31, 1975, to support this opinion. I suggested that 50 percent of stock market capital be invested in the funds and the remaining 50 percent be placed in cash (or bonds). This approach offered the long-term investor greater upside potential than the market at less downside risk, while earning a yield comparable to that of the typical common stock portfolio. Let's see how that advice turned out for the 28 months beginning January 1976.

Assuming that one had purchased equal dollar amounts of the four funds having superior risk/reward characteristics on December 31, 1975, here are the results:

	Closing prices		
	12/31/75	*4/28/78*	*Percent change*
Gemini Fund	$9.75	$22.125	+127
Income and Capital	4.625	6.50	+ 41
Leverage Fund	6.75	14.75	+118
Scudder Duo-Vest	4.625	8.00	+ 73
Average for the four funds			+ 90

A 50/50 combination between the funds and cash, as recommended for the conservative investor, would have appreciated by 45 percent compared to a gain of only 6 percent for the Standard & Poor's 500 stock index. How's that for an alternative to indexing? Or, an alternative to the strategies being touted by your favorite investment adviser?

4

MANAGING A CONVERTIBLE PORTFOLIO FOR HIGH-PROFIT POTENTIAL AT LOW RISK

The last two chapters presented superior alternatives to common stock portfolios for today's market. The closed-end convertible funds and dual-purpose funds, from Chapter 3, are ideal investments for those investors who want someone else to manage their money. This group of investors includes all who own mutual funds (load or no-load) plus those who retain the services of investment advisers or bank trust departments. All investors in this category should give serious consideration to switching their portfolios into these closed-end funds because of the risk/reward advantages. For those investors able and willing to manage their own portfolios or who have money managers who are skilled in convertibles, undervalued convertibles offer the optimum risk/reward opportunities. Carefully selected and managed portfolios of convertibles, in accordance with the guidelines to be presented in this chapter, should outperform even the discounted closed-end funds.

As stressed in Chapter. 2, the experienced investor should never purchase common stock without first checking to see whether there is a convertible security available that offers superior characteristics.

Since an undervalued convertible may often provide the same upside profit potential as its common stock but *at less downside risk,* it is surprising that so few investors are knowledgeable about the convertible securities market. Even among many sophisticated investors, few seldom have more than one or two convertibles in their portfolios. The reason for this anomaly is that investors may routinely check for convertibles on the stocks they like but do not take the next important step toward superior portfolio management. *They do not examine all the alternatives.*

FORD VERSUS GENERAL MOTORS

Suppose, for example, that one decides to invest in the automotive group and likes both Ford and General Motors. If the final selection were General Motors, there would be no choice but to buy the common stock since no convertible exists for GM. If, however, Ford were selected, the investor would find a convertible bond available that offers the same upside potential as Ford's common stock at *only half the downside risk.* The purchase of the convertible in this case would be the obvious alternative to buying common stock. But how about the investor who initially chose General Motors—for whatever reason? Since both companies were considered to be of equal quality, why not buy the Ford bond as a superior investment alternative to *either Ford common or General Motors common?* Note also that studies have shown that stocks within the same industry grouping tend to move together; thus, any advantage gained by an attempt to discriminate between companies in the same group may be a small one at best.

Exhibit 4–1 presents a graphical analysis of the Ford Motor 4⅞s of 1998 convertible bond. Note that for a 50-percent stock decline from $42 down to $21, the estimated loss for the bond is only 18 percent from 76 down to 62. And this assumes a near-term decline. Over the long term, the bond must ultimately be redeemed at 100 by the company whether the stock is selling at $21 or even lower.

OPPORTUNITIES IN CONVERTIBLES

There are over 500 actively traded convertibles (bonds and preferreds) listed on the New York Stock Exchange. From this large group, an investor can usually find about 100 different convertibles that offer significantly superior risk/reward characteristics compared to their underlying

Exhibit 4–1
Ford Motor 4⅞ s–'98 convertible bond, February 1978 (issue size, $158 million; bond converts into 18.04 shares)

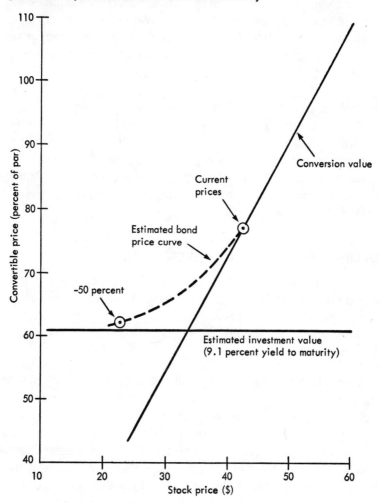

common stocks. These convertibles should *always* be purchased in lieu of their stocks. Since the selection is large and constantly changing, it is a relatively easy task to build a broadly diversified portfolio of undervalued convertibles, including participation in favored industry groups. The key is to first find the best convertibles and then evaluate the underlying stocks for the final decision. If one selects the stock first, like General Motors over Ford, he will frequently find that the company chosen doesn't have a convertible, let alone one that is undervalued.

Considering the large selection, noninstitutional size investors can build their total portfolios exclusively with undervalued convertibles—*and I strongly recommend doing just that.* They can thereby reduce downside risk without limiting upside profit potential. And in most cases, the current yield will exceed that of a comparable portfolio of common stocks —not to mention the lower commission expenses to purchase convertibles compared to stocks.

As you gain experience with convertibles, you will find that traditional techniques for selecting and managing stock portfolios can be replaced by a simpler set of analytical tools—tools that will permit you to make rational investment decisions without being influenced by your emotions. You will also spend much less time on fundamental or technical analysis of the companies involved while being surprised by the fact that you really can beat the market.

GUIDELINES FOR BUYING CONVERTIBLES

The following guidelines are the result of years of analytical study and actual experience with all kinds of markets. They should not be taken lightly as they will virtually assure that you will consistently outperform the market; an accomplishment that 95 percent of the professionals have been unable to achieve.

1. Determine your investment objective relative to the stock market as measured by a meaningful index such as the Standard & Poor's 500. For example, do you want to participate fully in an advancing market at say half the downside risk of the market? Or are you willing to give up some of the upside to attain even greater downside safety? This is a most important decision as it will govern your selection of which convertibles to buy and it will provide you with the means by which you can continually measure your progress.

2. Establish a procedure for evaluating potential candidates. If you want the full upside potential of the market, for instance, you will search for those undervalued convertibles trading close to their conversion value but not too far above their investment floor. Their underlying stocks should also have average or somewhat above average price volatility. Or the portfolio may be balanced by mixing convertibles on below average volatility stocks (like Ford Motor) with those having high volatility. This latter approach is recommended since it broadens your list to choose from. It also assures more consistent performance since at times the blue chip stocks

are in favor and at other times the market prefers the secondary issues.

3. Decide how much diversification you want. I would suggest 10 or more different issues in different industries.

4. Buy convertibles only on stocks that you are comfortable holding. Here you may apply your own fundamental or technical analysis to the underlying common stocks. Or you may wish to rely, as I do, on an investment advisory service with a proven track record.

5. Avoid convertibles trading at premiums over their conversion values and well above their call prices. You will lose the conversion premium and probably accrued interest also if the convertibles are called for redemption by the company.

SPECIFIC SELECTION PROCEDURES USING THE VALUE LINE OPTIONS AND CONVERTIBLES SERVICE

This single advisory service provides all the tools you need for building a portfolio of convertibles meeting the above guidelines. Assuming that you want a diversified portfolio that offers most of the upside potential of the stock market at less downside risk, here are the parameters.

1. **Value Line performance ranks.** Avoid poorly ranked securities by employing these ratings:

Underlying common stocks	− 3 or higher
Convertible bonds	− 3 or higher
Convertible preferreds	− 2 or higher

2. **Underlying stock volatility.** 75 minimum to 125 maximum. The portfolio should average near 100.

3. **Upside potential.** The convertible should advance 30 percent or more for a 50-percent stock advance (I may occasionally select one offering less upside if the downside risk is well below normal). The portfolio should average about 40 percent.

4. **Risk/reward ratio.** The risk/reward ratio compares the upside potential with the downside risk and is calculated as follows:

$$\text{Risk/reward ratio} = \frac{\text{Percent convertible advance}}{\text{50 percent stock advance}} \times \frac{\text{50 percent stock decline}}{\text{Percent convertible decline}}$$

This ratio should be 1.6:1 or higher for stock price changes of 50 percent (e.g., +50/−30 or +30/−18). The portfolio should average about 2:1 or higher.

5. **Current yield.** At today's interest rates, the minimum current yield for convertible bonds should be about 5.0 percent and for preferreds, 6.0 percent. The portfolio should average 6.0 percent or higher providing a cash flow advantage over the typical common stock portfolio.

By following the above selection procedures, you will gain a substantial edge over the stock market. Remember, the key to successful investing with convertibles is first to select those convertibles that are grossly undervalued. Then and only then should you evaluate the underlying common stocks before making your final decision. If you spend your time studying common stocks, you will probably never end up with a meaningful portfolio of convertibles.

UNDERVALUED CONVERTIBLES IN TODAY'S MARKET

Exhibits 4–2 and 4–3 present 20 undervalued convertible bonds and 14 preferreds that met my selection criteria in February 1978. The bonds and preferreds are shown separately for ease of reference, but in actual practice they would be listed in a common table. The following average characteristics for a portfolio of all 34 convertibles may be compared with the selection guidelines.

1. **Value Line performance ranks.** All underlying common stocks and their convertibles met the ranking selection criteria specified.
2. **Underlying stock volatility.** The average for the 34 positions was 93.4, or somewhat below the target of 100.
3. **Upside potential.** For a 50-percent stock advance, the convertibles were expected to advance about 42 percent. This compares to the target of 40 percent.
4. **Risk/reward ratio.** Dividing the 42 percent upside by 17.4 percent estimated downside risk for the convertibles (assuming a 50-percent stock decline) gives us a risk/reward ratio of 2.4; well above our portfolio objective of 2.0.
5. **Current yield.** The average for the 34 convertibles was 6.6 percent; compared with the 6.0 percent target.

All factors considered, the available convertibles in February 1978 offered substantial advantages over the stock market.

A "TYPICAL" CONVERTIBLE PRICE CURVE

The projected convertible price changes from Exhibits 4–2 and 4–3 may be averaged for preparing an estimated price curve for the "typical"

Exhibit 4–2
Undervalued convertible bonds (February 1978)

	Convertible description	Convertible price	Current yield	Stock volatility*	Projected percent change for the convertible for these changes in the price of the stock*			
					+50%	+25%	−25%	−50%
Amerace	5.000–92	72	7.0	75	+30%	+11%	−2%	−4%
Castle & Cooke	5.375–94	88	6.1	75	+40	+19	−11	−18
City Investing	7.500–90	91	8.2	110	+30	+14	−10	−16
Dayco	6.250–96	87	7.2	75	+40	+17	−10	−17
E-Systems	4.500–92	75	6.0	115	+35	+15	−9	−16
Federal National Mortgage	4.375–96	77	5.7	100	+50	+25	−14	−20
Ford Motor†	4.875–98	76	6.4	75	+50	+25	−14	−18
Harrah's	7.500–96	108	6.9	120	+45	+20	−11	−18
Hilton Hotels	5.500–95	91	6.1	120	+45	+20	−12	−20
Houston Industries‡	5.500–85	87	6.3	80	+30	+10	−2	−3
Lone Star Industries	5.125–93	76	6.7	100	+40	+17	−8	−11
Lucky Stores	6.750–00	100	6.7	85	+40	+16	−12	−19
National Can	7.000–01	110	6.4	85	+45	+22	−15	−24
Reading & Bates Offshore	5.500–88	96	5.8	125	+35	+16	−12	−21
Riegel Textile	5.000–93	77	6.5	85	+30	+14	−10	−16
Texas Commerce§	6.500–94	97	6.7	85	+40	+16	−7	−11
UV Industries	5.750–93	89	6.5	110	+45	+21	−11	−19
Wallace Murray	6.500–91	103	6.3	90	+50	+24	−15	−23
Wometco Enterprises	5.500–94	91	6.4	90	+40	+17	−11	−19
Zapata	4.750–88	78	6.1	115	+35	+17	−9	−17
Average for 20 convertibles			6.5	95	+40%	+18%	−10%	−17%

* Stock volatility data and price projections are by courtesy of Value Line.

† Trades as Ford Motor Credit.

‡ Trades as Houston Light & Power.

§ Trades as American General Insurance.

Exhibit 4–3
Undervalued convertible preferreds (February 1978)

	Convertible description	Convertible price	Current yield	Stock volatility*	Projected percent change for the convertible for these changes in the price of the stock*			
					+50%	+25%	−25%	−50%
Amerada Hess	$3.50	54.12	6.5	110	+45%	+21%	−11%	−18%
Arvin Industries	2.00	29.75	6.7	115	+50	+25	−16	−23
Carrier	1.86	28.00	6.6	105	+50	+24	−13	−21
Carter Hawley Hale ...	2.00	29.00	6.9	100	+45	+23	−12	−18
Chromalloy American ..	5.00	65.50	7.6	75	+45	+23	−9	−15
Colt Industries	4.25	63.75	6.7	95	+50	+24	−14	−21
Consolidated Foods ...	4.50	64.00	7.0	85	+35	+14	−7	−11
Foremost McKesson ...	1.80	28.38	6.3	75	+50	+25	−18	−25
IU International	1.25	18.25	6.8	85	+50	+25	−19	−25
Interpace	5.00	75.75	6.6	80	+50	+25	−16	−24
Kaiser Cement	2.50	35.50	7.0	95	+50	+24	−11	−18
Textron	2.08	29.00	7.2	90	+40	+17	−8	−13
Travelers	2.00	33.50	6.0	85	+40	+18	−13	−22
United States Gypsum ..	1.80	24.12	7.5	75	+35	+14	−4	−7
Average for 14 convertibles			6.8	91	+45%	+22%	−12%	−19%

* Stock volatility data and price projections are by courtesy of Value Line.

convertible. This typical price curve is shown by Exhibit 4–4 for stock price changes within a range of plus or minus 50 percent over the near term. This curve is useful for estimating performance of a diversified portfolio of undervalued convertibles under different stock market conditions as illustrated by the probability studies to follow.

Exhibit 4–4
The typical undervalued convertible

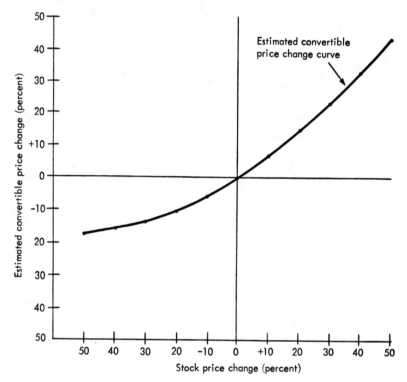

PROBABILITY ANALYSIS

Assuming that a diversified portfolio of undervalued convertibles will behave like the typical convertible of Exhibit 4–4, probability calculations for different market conditions are presented by Exhibit 4–5. As shown, a "bull market" assumes a market gain of 20 percent over a six-month period while a "bear market" assumes a 20-percent decline.

Looking first at the bull market calculations, the probability assumptions are that 1 of 10 underlying stocks will advance 40 percent; 2 of 10 will advance 30 percent, and so on. During a bear market, the opposite as-

Exhibit 4–5
Probability analysis for portfolios of undervalued convertibles held for six months

Stock price change	Convertible price change		Probability		
Bull markets					
+40%	+32%	×	0.1	=	+ 3.2%
+30	+23	×	0.2	=	+ 4.6
+20	+14	×	0.4	=	+ 5.6
+10	+ 7	×	0.2	=	+ 1.4
0	0	×	0.1	=	0
Expected profit for six months				=	+14.8%
Plus cash flow for six months				=	+ 3.3
Estimated total return for six months				=	+18.1%
Estimated annualized return				=	+36.2%
Sideways markets					
+20%	+14%	×	0.1	=	+ 1.4%
+10	+ 7	×	0.2	=	+ 1.4
0	0	×	0.4	=	0
−10	− 5	×	0.2	=	− 1.0
−20	− 9	×	0.1	=	− 0.9
Expected profit for six months				=	+ 0.9%
Plus cash flow for six months				=	+ 3.3
Estimated total return for six months				=	+ 4.2%
Estimated annualized return				=	+ 8.4%
Bear markets					
0%	0%	×	0.1	=	0%
−10	− 5	×	0.2	=	− 1.0
−20	− 9	×	0.4	=	− 3.6
−30	−13	×	0.2	=	− 2.6
−40	−16	×	0.1	=	− 1.6
Expected loss for six months				=	− 8.8%
Plus cash flow for six months				=	+ 3.3
Estimated total loss for six months				=	− 5.5%
Estimated annualized loss				=	−11.0%

sumptions are made. Admittedly, I have intentionally simplified the probability distributions for the purpose of clarity; however, the net results will not differ materially from more precise probability estimates.

These studies demonstrate that the total return for a portfolio of undervalued convertibles is expected to be significantly greater during a bull market move than the loss during a bear market. During a sideways or neutral market the total return from the convertible portfolio should about *double* that of a conventional stock portfolio.

A SIMPLIFIED PROBABILITY ANALYSIS

For making quick comparisons of one investment strategy with another, I have found the more simplified probability distribution of Exhibit 4–6

Exhibit 4–6
Simplified probability analysis for portfolios of undervalued convertibles held for six months

	Convertible price change		Probability		
Stock price change					
+40%	+32%	×	0.1	=	+ 3.2%
+20	+14	×	0.2	=	+ 2.8
0	0	×	0.4	=	0
−20	− 9	×	0.2	=	− 1.8
−40	−16	×	0.1	=	1.6
Expected profit for six months				=	+ 2.6%
Plus cash flow for six months				=	+ 3.3
Estimated total return for six months				=	+ 5.9%
Estimated annualized return				=	+11.8%

to be very useful. This table makes no assumptions about future market movements as did Exhibit 4–5.

The probability distribution figures from Exhibits 4–5 and 4–6 will be used frequently in the following chapters for comparing different strategies.

GUIDELINES FOR SELLING CONVERTIBLES

Since the convertibles selected are based on good common sense and mathematical relationships, the portfolio should be monitored along the same lines. There are also five basic guidelines I recommend for use in deciding when to sell a convertible. Whenever any of the following conditions are met, the convertible should be sold and replaced with one that meets the original selection criteria.

1. **The convertible rating drops to 4 or the stock rating to 5.** The Value Line system does seem to discriminate between issues with reasonable accuracy. You should, therefore, strive to keep the portfolio in better ranked positions and avoid the poorer ranks.

2. **The convertible's price advances.** As the market advances and the convertible moves well above its investment floor, you should take profits. For a 6.0 percent bond, for example, at a price of about

120 the risk/reward ratio has dropped so that the convertible no longer provides the downside protection you require. By replacing that convertible with a new one, you not only take profits, but also protect those profits by again buying convertibles which meet the original selection guidelines.

3. **The convertible will advance only 20 percent for a 50-percent stock move.** With the common stock declining, the convertible will lag as it approaches its investment value. The convertible has done its job. It has decreased less than the common and now takes on the characteristics of a straight debt instrument. Because the conversion premium has increased, the convertible will now trail behind the market on the upside. If the convertible will not advance 20 percent for a 50-percent stock move, it should be sold.

4. **The convertible becomes overpriced.** Any time a convertible becomes overpriced, it should be sold. We are working in an area where inefficiencies often develop. For no apparent reason, you may find the common going down and the convertible going up, or the common declining and the convertible lagging. In either case, the convertible may become overpriced and should be sold to take advantage of those inefficiencies.

5. **A marginal convertible may be sold to take advantage of an exceptional alternative.** Since you should continually strive to keep your portfolio in positions to participate in a market move, you may want to replace a marginal convertible that has not reached a point where a sell is indicated by the other guidelines with an exceptional alternative.

These guidelines provide a systematic framework for continually monitoring a portfolio to maintain it in the most advantageous risk/reward posture for participation in an up market whenever it occurs or for protection in a down market. What's more, you will never become "married" to any security you own. It is one of the few ways I know to take your emotions out of investing while increasing the odds in your favor.

A 16-MONTH "TRACK RECORD"

Beginning in December 1976, convertibles were purchased and managed for clients in accordance with previously specified guidelines. Although the holdings constituted the long side of SUPERHEDGE™ III portfolios, an advanced hedging strategy to be presented later, by themselves these convertibles permitted me to begin documenting a "track record" for those investors not wishing to employ hedging tactics.

A total of 63 convertibles were purchased during the period, and 28 were still held in April 1978 as shown by Exhibit 4–7. Clients that employed these securities earned a total net return (capital gains plus cash flow minus brokerage commissions) of about 26 percent compared to about a 4-percent net decline for the S&P 500 (dividends included).

Why did we beat the market by such a substantial amount as 30 percent?

Exhibit 4–7
Actual portfolio experience with undervalued convertibles

Convertible	Purchase data		Sale data*		Months held	Gain or loss
	Date	Price	Date	Price		
American Hoist	12–76	89	5–77	123	5	+38%
Continental Tel	12–76	82½	9–77	85	9	+ 3
Beech Aircraft	12–76	81	8–77	97	8	+20
Riegel Textile	12–76	77½	open	81	16	+ 5
Budd Company	12–76	92	1–78	142	13	+54
Wallace Murray	12–76	100	3–77	118	3	+18
Airco	12–76	96	6–77	105	6	+ 9
UV Industries	12–76	81	9–77	101	9	+25
North American Phillips	12–76	77½	6–77	77½	6	+ 0
Hilton Hotels	12–76	85½	6–77	87	6	+ 2
Parker Hannifan	12–76	74½	6–77	87	6	+17
Storer Broadcasting	12–76	85	5–77	86	5	+ 1
Federal National Mortgage	12–76	86	open	78½	16	− 9
White Consolidated	1–77	101½	6–77	106½	5	+ 5
Grumman Aircraft	1–77	61½	6–77	70	5	+14
Zapata	2–77	71	7–77	71½	5	+ 1
Houston Industries	2–77	94½	open	91	14	− 4
Citicorp	2–77	94½	3–78	75	13	−21
E-Systems	2–77	86	6–77	100	4	+16
Melville	2–77	89	4–77	94	14	+ 6
National Distillers	2–77	94½	11–77	87	9	− 8
Tesoro Petroleum	3–77	87½	7–77	87	4	− 1
Ogden	3–77	71	1–78	69	10	− 3
Sola Basic	3–77	90	5–77	120	2	+33
American Air Filter	3–77	96	5–77	102	2	+ 6
ITT	3–77	55½	2–78	48½	11	−13
Woolworth	4–77	34½	11–77	30	7	−13
Ford Motor	4–77	80	open	91	12	+14
FMC	4–77	75½	10–77	76½	6	+ 1
Oak Industries	5–77	70	5–77	72	1	+ 3
Dayco	5–77	93	open	90	11	− 3
Castle & Cooke	5–77	79	open	94½	11	+20
Athlone	5–77	28	3–78	29	10	+ 4
Insilco	5–77	18	open	17	10	− 6
Lear Sieger	6–77	41	2–78	38	8	− 7
Chase Manhattan Bank	6–77	72	1–78	71	7	− 7
Fairchild Industries	6–77	71½	12–77	78½	6	+10
Fruehauf	6–77	78½	1–78	74	7	− 6
Arvin Industries	7–77	29	open	30½	9	+ 5
UV Industries	7–77	90	open	96	9	+ 7

Exhibit 4–7 (continued)

Convertible	Purchase data		Sale data*		Months held	Gain or loss
	Date	Price	Date	Price		
American Hoist	8–77	96½	11–77	102	3	+ 6
Foremost McKesson	10–77	28	open	32	6	+14
Kaiser Cement	11–77	34	open	42	5	+24
Pennwalt	11–77	23½	open	23	5	− 2
Hilton Hotels	11–77	86½	open	109½	5	+27
Holiday Inns	11–77	24	4–77	27½	5	+15
E-Systems	12–77	83	open	82½	4	− 1
Harrah's	12–77	110	open	130	4	+18
Nat'l City Lines	12–77	66	open	67½	4	+ 2
Beech Aircraft	12–77	96	3–77	106	3	+10
Chromalloy	1–78	63	open	76	3	+21
Carrier	2–78	27½	4–77	34½	2	+25
Humana	2–78	92	open	101	2	+10
Textron	3–78	22	open	26	1	+18
Consolidated Foods	3–78	61½	open	62	1	+ 1
Carter Hawley Hale	3–78	28	open	31	1	+11
GAF	3–78	16½	open	17½	1	+ 6
Travelers	3–78	33½	open	37½	1	+12
McDermott	4–78	31½	open	31	0	− 2
Wallace Murray	4–78	110	open	110	0	0
Wometco Enterprises	4–78	96	open	103	0	+ 7
Western Airlines	4–78	79	open	89	0	+13
White Consolidated	4–78	85½	open	89½	0	+ 5

Averages (63 positions)	6.0	+ 7.6%
Convertible portfolio capital gain for 16 months (7.6 × 16/6.0 = 20.3)—interest and dividends not included .... =		+20.3%
S&P 500 change for 16 months since December 31, 1976 (107.46 down to 96.49)—dividends not included .... =		−10.2%
Convertible portfolio advantage over S&P 500 .... =		+30.5%

* April 28, 1978, closing prices for positions still held.

Note: Commissions were excluded from the convertible portfolio but were offset by a 2-percent higher yield than the S&P 500.

Part of our success must be related to the fact that we held convertibles on several potential takeover stocks during the year (e.g., American Hoist, Budd Company, and Sola Basic). But on the other hand, the portfolio included several convertibles on blue chip stocks that did not fare too well (e.g., Citicorp, ITT, and Woolworth). All in all, I believe that the exceptional performance was the combination of many different factors including our selection and portfolio management guidelines—guidelines that provide a substantial risk/reward advantage when setting up a portfolio plus the means to monitor the portfolio continually for optimum performance. We took profits, for example, on several rumored takeover situations that later pulled back when the takeovers failed to materialize.

WHAT ARE THE RISKS?

As with any investment strategy there are risks; both obvious risks as were illustrated and those that are more difficult to measure. The obvious (and measurable) risk is a bear market in which the convertibles decline in value along with their underlying common stocks. The less obvious risk is that the convertibles will decline by a greater amount than estimated. This might be caused by deteriorating fundamentals for the company (remember Penn Central) or rising long-term interest rates. Diversification and careful portfolio management will minimize the impact of an occasional large loser. As for rising interest rates, there is little that you can do to protect yourself from this event, although the continual monitoring of your portfolio will probably give you some offsetting profit-taking opportunities, even during severe bear markets.

CAN THE RISKS BE CONTROLLED?

The strategies to be presented in following chapters will show you how to remove virtually *all* risks from your convertible investment program by hedging with stocks and with listed put and call options. The next few chapters will cover traditional hedging tactics with listed options and common stocks and the final chapters will present the Superhedge™ strategies.

5

LISTED PUT AND CALL OPTIONS—IMPORTANT NEW TOOLS FOR PRUDENT INVESTING

There is probably no other area of the stock market as misunderstood as listed options. Even the majority of investors or speculators that actively trade in them just don't seem to understand them. They continually "follow the crowd" and thereby give away any market advantage they were hoping to achieve.

Put and call options have long been an important tool used by sophisticated investors, and with the creation of a listed option market in 1973, their use has been greatly expanded. In fact, many portfolios today employ option strategies exclusively.

Successful option trading is neither mysterious nor difficult. On the contrary, it is a skill you can develop with study and practice. My purpose here is to help you develop this skill by training you in new techniques and by teaching you to protect yourself from some of the dangers you will encounter along the way.

A comprehensive presentation of listed puts and calls is provided in the prospectus issued by the option exchanges. This prospectus, as well as other literature available from member brokerage firms, should be carefully studied before considering the use of options in your investment program. The option material to be presented in this book is not for beginners. Rather, it has been prepared for the sophisticated investor who has a firm knowledge of the stock market and experience with options. Only a limited amount of basic information is included, since such is readily available from other more conventional sources. My primary objective is to present advanced strategies for employing options that will allow you to seek above average performance in your investment program.

ADVANTAGES OF LISTED OPTIONS

Most advantages associated with listed options are directly related to the special features of this instrument which were unavailable in the conventional over-the-counter (OTC) options market. They are:

Standardized terms.

Secondary trading market.

Greater market depth.

Lower transaction costs.

Income tax advantages.

Listed options are currently available for a broad list of popular stocks. As shown by Exhibit 5–1, 219 stocks have listed calls, and 25 of these same stocks have listed puts. Future expansion plans include substantial additions to the put option list.

Exhibit 5–1
Listed put and call options, February 1978

Underlying stock	Stock symbol	Underlying stock	Stock symbol
AMF, Inc.	AMF	Avon Products	AVP*
ASA, Ltd.	ASA*	Babcock & Wilcox	BAW
Abbott Labs	ABT	Baker International	BKO
Aetna Life & Casualty	AET*	Bally Manufacturing	BLY
Allied Chemical	ACD	BankAmerica	BAM
Allis-Chalmers	AH*	Baxter Travenol Labs	BAX
Aluminum Co. of America	AA	Beatrice Foods	BRY
Amerada Hess	AHC*	Bethlehem Steel	BS
American Broadcasting	ABC*	Black & Decker	BDK
American Cyanamid	ACY	Blue Bell	BBL
American Electric Power	AEP	Boeing	BA
American Express	AXP	Boise Cascade	BCC
American Home Products	AHP	Bristol-Myers	BMY
American Hospital Supply	AHS	Brunswick	BC
American Telephone		Burlington Northern	BNI
& Telegraph	T	Burroughs	BGH
AMP, Inc.	AMP	CBS, Inc.	CBS
ASARCO	AR	Carrier	CRR*
Ashland Oil	ASH	Caterpillar Tractor	CAT
Atlantic Richfield	ARC	Champion International	CHA
Avnet	AVT		

* Put options are also available.

Exhibit 5–1 (*continued*)

Underlying stock	Stock symbol	Underlying stock	Stock symbol
Chase Manhattan	CMB	Greyhound	G
Citicorp	FNC	Gulf & Western	GW
City Investing	CNV	Gulf Oil	GO
Clorox	CLX	Halliburton	HAL
Coastal States Gas	CGP	Hercules	HPC
Coca Cola	KO	Heublein	HBL*
Colgate-Palmolive	CL	Hewlett-Packard	HWP
Combustion Engineering	CSP	Hilton Hotels	HLT
Commonwealth Edison	CWE	Holiday Inns	HIA
Communications Satellite	CQ	Homestake Mining	HM
Consolidated Edison	ED	Honeywell	HON*
Continental Oil	CLL*	Household Finance	HFC
Continental Telephone	CTC	Houston Oil & Minerals	HOI
Control Data	CDA	Howard Johnson	HJ
Corning Glass Works	GLW*	Hughes Tool	HT*
Deere	DE	INA Corp.	INA
Delta Air Lines	DAL	Inexco Oil	INX*
Diamond Shamrock	DIA	International Business	
Digital Equipment	DEC	Machines	IBM*
Disney	DIS	International Flavors	
Dr. Pepper	DOC	& Fragrances	IFF
Dow Chemical	DOW	International Harvester	HR
Dresser Industries	DI	International Minerals	
Dupont	DD	& Chemicals	IGL
Duke Power	DUK	International Paper	IP
Eastern Gas & Fuel	EFU	International Telephone	
Eastman Kodak	EK*	& Telegraph	ITT
El Paso	ELG	ITEL Corp.	I
Engelhard Minerals		Johns-Manville	JM
& Chemicals	ENG	Johnson & Johnson	JNJ
Evans Products	EVY	Joy Manufacturing	JOY
Exxon	XON	K Mart	KM
Federal National Mortgage	FNM	Kennecott Copper	KN
Federated Department		Kerr McGee	KMG
Stores	FDS	Levi Strauss	LVI*
Firestone Tire & Rubber	FIR	Lilly (Eli & Co.)	LLY
First Charter Financial	FCF	Litton Industries	LIT
Fleetwood Enterprises	FLE	Loews	LTR
Fluor	FLR	Louisiana Land	
Ford Motor	F	& Exploration	LLX
Freeport Minerals	FT	Louisiana-Pacific	LPX
GAF Corp.	GAF	Lucky Stores	LKS
General Dynamics	GD	MGIC Investment	MGI
General Electric	GE	MAPCO, Inc.	MDA
General Foods	GF	Marriott	MHS
General Motors	GM*	McDermott (J. Ray & Co.)	MDE
General Telephone		McDonalds	MCD
& Electric	GTE	McDonnell Douglas	MD
Georgia Pacific	GP	Merck	MRK
Gillette	GS	Merrill Lynch	MER
Goodyear Tire & Rubber	GT	Mesa Petroleum	MSA*
Grace, W. R.	GRA	Middle South Utilities	MSU
Great Western Financial	GWF		

* Put options are also available.

Exhibit 5–1 (concluded)

Underlying stock	Stock symbol	Underlying stock	Stock symbol
Minnesota Mining		Scott Paper	SPP
& Manufacturing	MMM	Seaboard Coast Line	SCI
Mobil	MOB	Searle, G. D.	SRL
Monsanto	MTC	Sears Roebuck	S
Motorola	MOT	Signal Companies	SGN
NCR Corp.	NCR	Simplicity Pattern	SYP
NL Industries	NL	Skyline	SKY
National Distillers		Southern Co.	SO
& Chemicals	DR	Sperry Rand	SY
National Semiconductor	NSM	Standard Oil Co. California	SD
Northwest Airlines	NWA	Standard Oil Co. Indiana	SN
Northwest Industries	NWT*	Sterling Drug	STY
Norton Simon	NSI	Sun Co.	SUN
Occidental Petroleum	OXY	Syntex	SYN
Owens-Illinois	OI	TRW, Inc.	TRW
PPG Industries	PPG	Tandy	TAN
Penney, J. C.	JCP	Teledyne	TDY
Pennzoil	PZL	Tenneco	TGT
PepsiCo	PEP	Tesoro Petroleum	TSO
Perkin-Elmer	PKN	Texaco	TX
Pfizer	PFE	Texas Instruments	TXN
Phelps Dodge	PD	Texasgulf	TG
Philip Morris	MO	Tiger International	TGR
Phillips Petroleum	P	Transamerica	TA
Pitney-Bowes	PBI	Travelers	TIC
Pittston	PCO*	UAL, Inc.	UAL
Polaroid	PRD	Union Carbide	UK
Procter & Gamble	PG	Union Oil Co. California	UCL
RCA Corp.	RCA	Union Pacific	UNP
Ralston Purina	RAL	United States Steel	X
Raytheon	RTN	United Technologies	UTX
Reserve Oil and Gas	RVO*	Upjohn	UPJ
Revlon	REV*	Virginia Electric & Power	VEL
Reynolds (R. J.) Industries	RJR	Walter, Jim	JWC
Reynolds Metals	RLM	Warner-Lambert	WLA
Rite Aid	RAD	Western Union	WU
Rockwell International	ROK	Westinghouse	WX*
Safeway Stores	SA	Weyerhaeuser	WY
Sambo's Restaurants	SRI	Williams Companies	WMB
Santa Fe International	SAF*	Woolworth	Z
Schering-Plough	SGP*	Xerox	XRX
Schlumberger	SLB	Zenith Radio	ZE

* Put options are also available.

Standardized terms

Each option has four fixed expiration months, e.g., January, April, July, and October. Trading in options of a particular expiration month begins nine months earlier so that at any given time there are options trading with three different expiration months. All options expire on the Saturday immediately following the third Friday of the month. Trading ceases the previous Friday.

Exercise prices are normally fixed at 5-point intervals for stocks trading below 50, at 10-point intervals for stocks trading between 50 and 200, and at 20-point intervals for stocks above 200. When trading begins in a new expiration month, the exercise price for the option is fixed at a dollar-per-share figure close to the current market price of the underlying common stock.

If significant price movements take place in an underlying stock between the introduction of new expiration months, additional options with new exercise prices may be opened for trading. Consequently, the investor in listed puts and calls is offered a choice of exercise prices and related premiums having widely different risk/reward characteristics. What's more, these variations permit the alert investor to take advantage of overpriced and undervalued options resulting from the day-to-day supply/demand imbalances of the marketplace.

Secondary trading market

The most important new feature of listed options is a secondary market in which existing options are freely traded. This innovation clearly sets listed options apart from OTC options, which have virtually no resalability. In the absence of a secondary trading market, an option holder must exercise the option (or sell it at its salvage value) to realize any profit. The holder of such an OTC option has almost no opportunity to realize additional value for the length of time remaining until the option's expiration date. Likewise, the seller of an OTC option has little or no opportunity to liquidate his position before the expiration date.

On the other hand, holders of listed options have liquid, marketable instruments. They can close out their positions in the secondary market at any time. And after buying a put or a call, the investor can continuously follow its price as it rises or falls in conjunction with the price movements of the underlying stock.

Similarly, sellers of listed options are able to redeem their obligations through purchases in the secondary trading market.

Market depth

The popularity of listed options has resulted in a market depth that never existed in the over-the-counter market. This depth permits trading in relatively large volume without significantly disrupting the market. In fact, certain institutional investors have purchased large numbers of calls with the intention of exercising them, as a superior alternative to the outright purchase of the underlying common stocks.

Sellers of listed calls who own the underlying common stocks (or convertibles) may be reasonably sure that future calls can be sold on a continuing basis without having to liquidate the long side of their positions each time and search for other situations that are in demand by buyers.

Lower transaction costs

The option exchanges, which have commission structures similar to other securities exchanges, offer significant saving compared to the price spreads experienced in the negotiated OTC options market. Even more important, profitable options can be sold in the secondary market at regular commission rates without incurring the extraordinarily high commission expense of the OTC exercise process.

If a put or a call is likely to be exercised by the holder, the seller may buy it back at nominal expense instead of paying the higher commissions on the purchase or sale of common stocks in response to the exercise notice.

Income tax advantages

The present tax treatment of the sale of call options has corrected a tax disadvantage that applied to writers of listed calls through September 1976. Those early writers incurred ordinary income if their calls expired worthless or were repurchased at a profit. During bear markets (remember 1974), these early writers experienced capital losses on stock holdings but were required to pay full income taxes on profits earned from the calls sold. New tax legislation changed the ruling by treating profits or losses on call options sold as a short-term capital gain or loss, as with conventional short selling—and writing a call option *really* is like a short sale. The new laws permit sophisticated writers to offset short-term bear market profits on call options by taking capital losses on underlying stocks, thereby avoiding excessive taxes.

In spite of this tax law change, brokerage firms and others still advertise option writing as a means for the serious investor to earn extra "income." They obviously know that "earning extra income" sounds much more appealing and conservative than "earning extra profits by selling short."

BASIC OPTION STRATEGIES

The two exhibits to be discussed shortly are built around six basic investment strategies. Listed in descending order from the most bullish to the most bearish, they are:

Buy 100 shares of stock.

Buy one call option.

Sell one put option (uncovered).

Sell one call option (uncovered).

Buy one put option.

Sell short 100 shares of stock.

All tactics with puts and calls involve one or more of these six basic strategies. If you understand the risk/reward characteristics of each, you should have no trouble evaluating any other suggested strategy— whether it be a strip, a strap, or whatever other complex tactics the investment community might dream up to complicate your life and to enrich its bank accounts.

Exhibit 5–2 illustrates the risk/reward characteristics for the six basic strategies based on these parameters.

1. The common stock is trading at $50.
2. Six-month puts and calls having $50 exercise prices are both trading at $5 (10 percent premiums).
3. Commissions and dividends are excluded to simplify the illustrations.

As shown in the exhibit, the outcome of each strategy at expiration of the option is given for a stock price range between $30 and $70. This permits us conveniently to illustrate the potential risk and reward for each strategy. For example, the conventional strategy of purchasing common stock (strategy 1) offers a possible loss of $2,000 versus a potential gain of $2,000. The purchase of a call option (strategy 2), an alternative to buying common stock, limits the downside risk to the $500

Exhibit 5–2
Alternate strategies with listed puts and calls
Assumptions: 1. Stock is trading at $50.
                2. Six-month puts and calls, having $50 exercise prices, are both
                     trading at $5 (10 percent premiums).
                3. Commissions and dividends are excluded.

		Prices at expiration date			
Stock		30	40	50	60	70
Call		0	0	0	10	20
Put		20	10	0	0	0
Bullish strategies						
1.	Buy 100 shares of stock	(2,000)	(1,000)	0	1,000	2,000
1a.	Buy one call and					
	sell one put	(2,000)	(1,000)	0	1,000	2,000
2.	Buy one call	(500)	(500)	(500)	500	1,500
2a.	Buy 100 shares and					
	buy one put	(500)	(500)	(500)	500	1,500
3.	Sell one put	(1,500)	(500)	500	500	500
3a.	Buy 100 shares and					
	sell one call	(1,500)	(500)	500	500	500
Bearish strategies						
4.	Sell one call	500	500	500	(500)	(1,500)
4a.	Short 100 shares and					
	sell one put	500	500	500	(500)	(1,500)
5.	Buy one put	1,500	500	(500)	(500)	(500)
5a.	Short 100 shares and					
	buy one call	1,500	500	(500)	(500)	(500)
6.	Short 100 shares of stock	2,000	1,000	0	(1,000)	(2,000)
6a.	Buy one put and					
	sell one call	2,000	1,000	0	(1,000)	(2,000)
Neutral strategies						
a.	Buy 100 shares and					
	sell two calls	(1,000)	0	1,000	0	(1,000)
b.	Short 100 shares and					
	sell two puts	(1,000)	0	1,000	0	(1,000)
c.	Sell one straddle	(1,000)	0	1,000	0	(1,000)

premium paid while offering the full upside potential of the stock, minus the premium ($2,000 − $500 = $1,500). Of course, if the stock remained unchanged, the call option buyer would also lose the entire $500 premium while the stock buyer would suffer no loss.

The major purpose of Exhibit 5–2 is to demonstrate that for every basic strategy there is an alternative—you should never use one without first considering the other. Let us briefly review each of the six basic strategies and their alternatives. Guidelines will be developed for helping you determine which alternative offers the most favorable risk/reward prospects.

BULLISH STRATEGIES

1 versus 1a. The risk/reward characteristics of buying common stock (1) are obvious to everyone, but the alternate strategy of buying a call and selling a put (1a) may offer advantages. First, on the assumption that the premium received for selling the put is the same as the premium paid for buying the call, there would be no net debit charged to your account—compared to a debit of $5,000 for the purchase of stock. The collateral required for margining the naked put might earn a greater yield than that paid on the common. Second, commission expenses for the put and call alternative might be lower than for the purchase of common stock. Note that these advantages would apply regardless of whether overall option premiums are high or low as long as the relationship between the put and call premiums is as indicated.

2 versus 2a. The alternative to the simple purchase of a call option (2) is the purchase of 100 shares of stock plus one put option (2a). The call option strategy will normally be the best unless the common stock is a high-dividend payer and/or the put premium is substantially lower than the call premium.

3 versus 3a. The sale of an uncovered put option (3) is an excellent alternative to the conventional sale of a covered call against the under-lying stock (3a)—possibly greater yield on the collateral used for selling the naked put versus the dividend paid on the stock, plus lower commission expenses.

BEARISH STRATEGIES

4 versus 4a. The sale of a put against 100 shares of stock sold short (4a) will seldom offer superior advantages to the simple sale of an un-covered call option (4) since dividends (if any) must be paid on the stock sold short as well as higher commission expenses.

5 versus 5a. The simple purchase of a put option (5) will normally offer advantages for bear market profits over the complex strategy of shorting 100 shares of stock against a call option (5a)—no dividends paid on stock sold short plus lower commissions.

6 versus 6a. The more sophisticated strategy of buying a put and sell-ing a call option (6a) will normally be more advantageous than the short sale of common stock (6), especially if the put premium is lower than the call premium and if the stock pays a dividend.

As noted in the above discussion for bullish and bearish strategies, the dividend paid on the common stock and the premium difference between the put and call are important factors to consider when evaluating the available alternatives. Exhibit 5–3 summarizes these considerations

Exhibit 5–3
Comparison of alternate strategies with listed puts and calls

Put premium versus call premium ⟶	Stock pays no dividend			Stock dividend equals money market rate		
	Lower	Same	Higher	Lower	Same	Higher
Bullish strategies						
1 or 1a	*	1a	1a	1	Either	1a
2 or 2a	*	2	2	2a	Either	2
3 or 3a	*	3	3	3a	Either	3
Bearish strategies						
4 or 4a	4	Either	4a	4	4	*
5 or 5a	5	Either	5a	5	5	*
6 or 6a	6a	Either	6	6a	6a	*
Neutral strategies						
a, b, or c	a or c*	b or c	b	a	a or c	b or c*

* The best strategy will depend on the precise difference between put and call premiums relative to interest earned on the collateral used to carry the positions.

and indicates the favored strategy depending on these factors. Commission expense differences are less important and are excluded, but they could tip the scales if all other factors are equal.

NEUTRAL STRATEGIES

Exhibits 5–2 and 5–3 also include neutral strategies for optimizing return on investment during a sideways market movement—the most common being the sale of two calls against 100 shares of stock (the variable or ratio hedge). Depending on the stock's yield versus money market rates and the difference between put and call premiums, the other alternatives may be better.

NORMAL PREMIUMS FOR LISTED OPTIONS

The concept of normal premiums for puts and calls is an important tool employed by most successful investors in listed options. By definition, a normal premium is the amount of money that option buyers or sellers should pay or receive to compensate them fairly for market risk.

Option premiums are primarily related to: the common stock's yield, the price volatility of the common stock, the length of time the option has to run, and the stock price relative to the option's exercise price. Complex mathematical formulas are available for computing fair values based on these and other variables. A discussion of these formulas is beyond the scope of this book, but you should always refer to an advisory service that provides this information before making a buy or sell decision. Remember, option buyers should seldom pay more than the normal premium and sellers should seldom accept less. Otherwise, they are giving away the opportunity to earn a fair profit relative to the risks assumed.

When listed options first began trading, option premiums were much too high relative to normal premium calculations. This was obviously caused by a shortage of sellers. As more sellers came into the market, the market became reasonably efficient and option premium levels have dropped. Within this efficient market framework, however, day-to-day supply/demand pressures do create undervalued options for purchase and overpriced options for sale. This situation will *always* exist as we have experienced with the convertible securities market.

6

WHEN NOT TO WRITE CALL OPTIONS

The widely acclaimed ability to attain high returns at low risk by writing call options against common stock has to rank as one of Wall Street's worst financial fantasies. Yet, the concept is being marketed aggressively to those investors seeking high current income who can ill afford the inherent risks of an option writing program.

The most popular option strategy by far has been the sale of covered calls. Numerous advisory services and most brokerage firms provide a steady flow of recommended covered writes to the investment public. Many offer elaborate computerized printouts to aid in selection and monitoring. Yes, call writing has become a very popular game.

Can serious investors sell call options against common stock in today's market and expect to receive an above average return on their investment capital? *I don't think so!* It is at best a break-even strategy and probably a losing one.[1] Call premiums are just too low!

From *How the Experts Beat the Market* I quote "Except for those using the sophisticated tools available, option sellers generally have been disappointed with their performance. They have not received the 20, 30, or 40 percent returns on their portfolios promised by brokers and advisory services. Most, in fact, have struggled to just break even! But why should they have expected to do much better than break even? Are op-

---

[1] I define "break-even" as equaling the return from risk-free money market instruments.

tion buyers so naive as to permit unreasonably large returns to the sellers? I doubt it!"

Since the time the material for *How the Experts Beat the Market* was prepared in 1975, six-month call premiums have plummeted from about 12½ percent down to 7½ percent. This 5-percent differential for six months means that covered writing in today's market will return 10 *percent less* per annum than the strategy did previously. Ratio writing has suffered an even greater decline in potential return. The typical 2-for-1 ratio hedge offers *20 percent less than before.*

Will premiums return to their former lofty levels in the near future? Probably not! Overall, premium levels are primarily determined by supply/demand pressures in the marketplace. At the present time, there are far too many new sellers seeking those high returns that others supposedly earned in previous years. A future bull market will probably bring more buyers into the option market, but in the meantime, huge pools of money have been formed for writing calls, including several new mutual funds.

I expect these funds (and other late entrants into the game) ultimately to underperform the stock market leading to future net redemption of their shares. However, it will probably take a complete stock market cycle (or two) to "shake them out" as it is extremely difficult for most investors to evaluate the performance (good or bad) of an option writing program. For example, over the near term, a sideways or higher market should produce sufficient results to satisfy most shareholders. On the downside, losses during the bear phase of a market cycle might be "explained away" on the basis that they were less than the losses of unhedged portfolios managed by others. It may take five or more years for their expected poor track records to have meaningful value to the investment public.

It was difficult for most investors to earn above average profits in earlier years when premiums were higher, and it's virtually impossible at today's lower premium levels. Common sense tells us (or detailed probability studies if you prefer) that the option writer no longer has an edge over the buyer. Writing calls against common stock has become one of the worst investment strategies.

For example, let us assume that a covered writer sells a six-month call at 10 percent premium against 100 shares of a nondividend-paying stock trading at $50, and having average price volatility. As each call expires, a new six-month call at 10 percent premium will be sold. We will also assume that the stock trades in a relatively narrow price range of between $40 and $60 over a two-year period. Now, I have heard brokers and investors alike claim that this strategy will return 20 percent per year on one's investment—doesn't 10 percent every six months equal a 20-percent annual rate of return? It may in fantasyland, but in the real world of investing, the potential results from a continuous covered writing program for the market conditions described may be estimated as shown in Exhibit 6–1.

Exhibit 6–1

Six-month cycle	Security	Beginning price	Ending price	Profit or (loss) Stock	Call
Stock goes from 50 to 40	Stock	$50	$40	($1,000)	—
	Call	5	0	—	$500
Stock goes from 40 to 50	Stock	40	50	1,000	—
	Call	4	10	—	(600)
Stock goes from 50 to 60	Stock	50	60	1,000	—
	Call	5	10	—	(500)
Stock goes from 60 to 50	Stock	60	50	(1,000)	—
	Call	6	0	—	600
Net profit or loss for two years (excluding commissions)				$ 0	$ 0

If you are an option seller or are considering the sale of call options as one of your investment tools, please take a few minutes to study this analysis. It may save you thousands of dollars and much disappointment if its impact is fully understood and appreciated.

Promised returns of 15 percent and higher from a conventional call-selling program against common stocks are simply financial fantasy! In today's world, above average investment performance from an option-selling program can be achieved *only by employing the most sophisticated tools available*. These tools *are* available to serious investors if they are willing to do their homework and to discard all the time-consuming, irrelevant trivia that is continually pushed at them by those wanting commission or subscription dollars. These tools will be fully disclosed in the following chapters.

In spite of today's lower premiums, there *are* ways to employ call option selling with expectations for an above average return—but not against common stocks. The next chapter will illustrate their use with undervalued convertibles, and later chapters will develop even more advanced strategies. For those who still insist on selling calls against common stock, for whatever reasons, here are ten do's and don'ts to help you improve your performance.

1. DO recognize that covered call writing is a *bullish* strategy. You really do want the underlying common stock to advance in price as was shown by the analysis earlier in this chapter. It's surprising how many call writers actually hope that their stocks don't advance so as to avoid losing money on the calls sold. Exhibit 6–2 illus-

Exhibit 6–2
Tesoro Petroleum covered hedge, July 1977 (excluding commissions and dividends)

Stock price   = $1,500
Minus call premium = − 125
Net investment   = $1,375

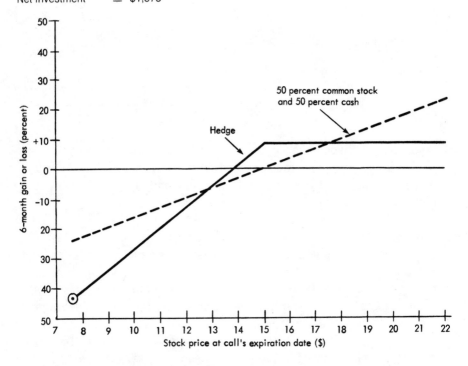

trates a covered hedge in Tesoro Petroleum (available during July 1977) assuming the stock is at the call's exercise price of 15 and that six-month calls are sold at 8½ percent premium for 1¼ ($125). Note that the risk/reward posture is roughly comparable to placing 50 percent of your capital in the stock unhedged and the other 50 percent in cash. The hedge offers more return between stock prices of $12¾ and $17¾ but at a greater risk, or less return, beyond that range.

2. DO evaluate potential risk as well as reward. The simple calculation of a downside break-even price is an inadequate measurement of risk. It's the potential loss after the break-even price is penetrated that is most important. Exhibit 6–2 shows that the break-even price for the Tesoro Petroleum position is an 8½ percent decline to $13¾. But if the stock were to drop 50 percent to $7½, the loss on the covered hedge would be a substantial 45 percent in only six months (90 percent annualized!) Also, be sure to recognize that common stocks *can* fall 50 percent or more in relatively short periods of time. The Tesoro example was actually used to illustrate risk in the August 1977 issue of *Advance Investment Strategies*™.[2] As if the example were selected by a "crystal ball," Tesoro Petroleum promptly plunged 50 percent to $7½ by the end of the year, and Tesoro was not alone. Bethlehem Steel dropped from $40 to $18, Dow Chemical from $44 to $25 and Eastman Kodak from $87 to $49 during 1977. These were all popular stocks used in covered writing programs. They declined substantially in a market downturn relatively mild compared with other bear markets of recent memory.

3. DO recognize that a diversified portfolio of covered option positions is *expected* to perform differently than a single position. For example, a booklet titled "The Merrill Lynch Guide to Writing Options" stated that a covered writing program can be expected to produce a yield of about 15 percent a year in stable or rising markets. That statement may be true during bull markets when all positions are rising, but it is totally incorrect for stable markets when some stocks are rising while others are falling. For example, if you owned two different hedge positions, as illustrated by Exhibit 6–2 for Tesoro Petroleum, and one stock advanced 50 percent while the other declined 50 percent, the "average" for the two stocks would be unchanged. But, the 9-percent profit (for six months) earned on the winner compares to a 45-percent loss on the loser. The net loss on your portfolio during this "stable" market period would be 18 percent for six months or a 36-percent annualized loss! I fail to see where the +15 percent Merrill Lynch talks about exists in that 36-percent potential loss.

---

[2] *Advanced Investment Strategies*™ is an investment advisory service published monthly by Thomas C. Noddings and Associates, Inc., 135 S. LaSalle St., Chicago, Ill. 60603.

The Tesoro example was obviously exaggerated to illustrate the point. For a diversified portfolio of 10 or more different positions, you can probably expect to earn about half the maximum potential during a typical sideways market assuming that no stock in your portfolio declines by more than about 20 percent. If you are unlucky enough to be holding a 50-percent loser, like Tesoro Petroleum during the last half of 1977, you will probably do no better than break even for the six-month period and may be down several percentage points. Remember that your winners will provide only modest profits, but that losses can be very large.

4. DON'T expect defensive strategies to improve your overall performance. It's true that "rolling down" options and other defensive maneuvers may help avoid big losers. But these trading tactics are certain to create more small losers and fewer winners from the natural and expected "whipsawing" movements of the stock market. Too much trading activity in any investment program will enrich your broker's bank account, but rarely yours.

5. DON'T sell deep-in-the-money calls (or even those that are modestly in-the-money). This strategy will simply tie up your capital while offering little or no profit opportunity. It is much like selling stock short against the box, a no-risk, no-profit tactic that should only be used for deferring taxes into the following year.

6. DON'T use margin. Repeat . . . DON'T USE MARGIN! Exhibit 6–3 illustrates that the break-even price of $13¾ for the Tesoro Petroleum hedge position on margin is the same as for the nonmargined hedge. But at a stock price of $7½, the six-month loss is substantially increased—from 45 percent up to 100 percent (200 percent annualized!) Exhibit 6–3 also shows that writing covered calls on margin can be much riskier than the *very bullish* strategy of owning the stock unhedged. Yet, many conservative investors employ margin when writing call options believing that it is a low-risk strategy.

7. DON'T blindly follow computerized recommendations giving the best covered writes assuming the calls are exercised. These reports seldom consider downside risk (other than the simplistic calculation of the downside break-even price), and they almost always favor the higher volatility stocks, thus exposing your capital to substantial losses in a bear market.

8. DON'T allow your stocks to be called away. The commission expenses to let your stock be called and to replace it with another stock will seriously erode your capital over time. Normally, it's best

Exhibit 6–3
Tesoro Petroleum covered hedge on margin, July 1977 (excluding commissions, dividends, and margin interest)

Stock on 50% margin = $750
Minus call premium = −125

Net investment = $625

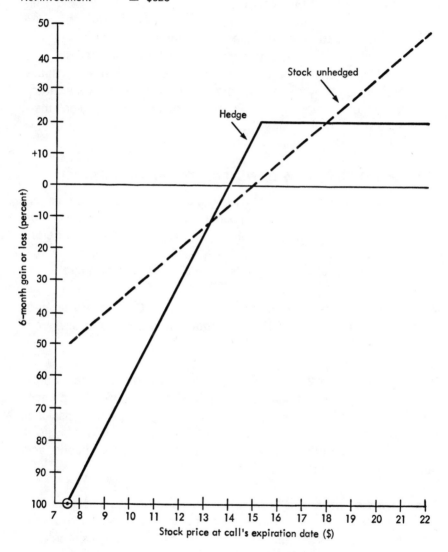

to buy back the in-the-money call and to write another call having a higher exercise price. Note that certain strategies (e.g., selling deep-in-the-money calls) recommended by some brokers seem to be intentionally designed to have your stocks called away so that the extra commissions may be obtained.

9. DON'T sell undervalued options. Many writers are actually unaware of what a fair market price for the option should be. They "give away" any hope of achieving a fair rate of return from their option writing program.

10. DON'T be fooled by "last year's" track record. If someone indicates a 15-percent potential return from an option writing program and shows a 15-percent actual return during the previous year to support this objective, that might be completely unacceptable. To achieve a given rate of return over the long term, you must usually earn substantially more than that in good years. For any "track record" to be meaningful, it must cover at least one full stock market cycle.

THE OPTION FUNDS—WIDOWS AND ORPHANS BEWARE!

Since selling calls is a major tool we use with many of our hedging strategies, we are more than just a little concerned that the new option funds mentioned earlier will depress call premiums even further. So before presenting our advanced hedging strategies, let us examine these new mutual funds so as to provide a reference point for our own strategies.

Who are they?   The present group of five are: Colonial, Federated, Kemper, Oppenheimer, and Putnam. They range upward in size from $50 million each.

What do they charge?   All are load funds charging 9.3 percent above net asset value for investments up to $10,000. In addition, management fees and miscellaneous expenses (excluding brokerage commissions) will run about 1 to 1½ percent each year. The 9.3 percent load by itself has already extracted over $25 million from the investment public, and there is more to come.

What have they promised?   In spite of common sense and published probability studies to the contrary, these funds are promising an above average total return (typically 12 to 15 percent) at below average risk. The 12- to 15-percent "total return" is supposedly to consist of about 4 percent from dividends and the balance from *short-term trading profits!*

How have they done so far?   It's too soon for the funds to have developed meaningful track records so we must wait another year or two. One fund was *extremely pleased* to issue its August 30, 1977, report advising that it had lost only 1.7 percent for the two months since its inception (a 10-percent annualized loss!). As of December 31, 1977, the same fund was still only back to about even. This fund had to gain the full 12 percent during the first half of 1978 to earn its 12-percent minimum objective for its first year of operation. Obviously, this was a difficult, if not impossible task, for any call writing program, even under ideal conditions. As of March 31, 1978, the net assets of the fund, plus dividends previously distributed to shareholders, were still about unchanged.

What do I think these funds will do? I believe these funds will achieve only their 12- to 15-percent objective during the bull phase of a market cycle, and then only if they don't trade their positions too frequently. They *will do worse* in a sideways market, and they *will be losers* in bear markets. Over a market cycle, I doubt that they will even match the average return from risk-free money market instruments.

What are the tax considerations? The strategies being employed by these option funds will seldom produce long-term capital gains, thus any earnings achieved are subject to full income taxes. In fact, in a down market they will probably earn sizeable short-term profits on the options sold versus unrealized losses on their common stocks. Since they are required to pay out these short-term gains, the investor could end up paying taxes while the total net asset value of his shares has declined. The previously mentioned fund that broke even during the later half of 1977 actually paid out a $0.61 dividend at the end of the year (4.5 percent for six months). This probably pleased most shareholders; however, their net asset value was reduced by the dividend. So, in reality, the shareholders ended up paying full income taxes on what amounted to a return of their capital. Their net worth declined while the fund "broke even." Hardly a winning strategy in my opinion.

I am obviously most negative on the prospects for these option writing funds, and frankly, I feel that the public has been "ripped off" by the investment community. And I am not completely alone. In the October 1977 issue of *Mutual Funds Scoreboard,* editor Yale Hirsch asked, "On what basis are brokers recommending these funds? And what will so much money chasing options do to option premiums?" Also, an article on covered call option writing in the December 15, 1977, issue of *Forbes* was aptly titled "Suckers Wanted."

So much for the "bad guys." How can *you* employ call option writing strategies in today's market with expectations for an above average return at below average risk?

AVOID COMMON STOCKS WHEN SELLING CALLS!

My answer to today's lower premium level is to sell only call options that are normally priced (or overpriced) *against securities that are undervalued.* As shown in Chapters 2 and 4, convertible bonds and preferreds are frequently overlooked in the marketplace and are excellent investment instruments for gaining an edge on the stock market. So, call options may be sold against *undervalued* convertibles, but they should *never* be sold against common stocks unless premiums return to their former excessively high levels.

The individual writer of call options can gain a significant advantage over the "pros" since he can employ convertibles while they cannot. The mutual funds and other institutional investors must maintain their underlying common stocks in custody at a bank, which in return issues escrow receipts to the Option Clearing Corporation. The system is not presently capable of employing escrow receipts against convertible securities. But even should the system be changed in the future, convertibles do not provide the liquidity that the institutions require for investing their huge pools of capital as I pointed out in Chapter 2. That's too bad for them, but very good for us.

7

A SUPERIOR CALL OPTION WRITING STRATEGY

Just as sophisticated investors prefer undervalued convertibles as a superior alternative to common stocks in a conventional investment program, experienced hedgers will seldom use stocks as their under-lying securities when selling call options. The large number of listed calls presently trading provides many opportunities for selecting under-valued convertibles for the long side of the hedge. A diversified port-folio of ten or more positions can normally be achieved within a reason-able period of time.

Common stocks are employed in call option hedges by the sophisticated investor *only* when the calls are *overpriced*. However, even the careful selection of overpriced options does not assure superior long-term per-formance. When the calls expire, the probabilities are that new calls will be only normally valued. Hedgers are then faced with two choices, and both are bad. They may write normally valued calls, or they may sell their stock and search for another opportunity that offers a call option that is overpriced. The first choice amounts to little more than "trading dollars," and the latter approach will likely eat up too many commission dollars relative to invested capital. These problems have always existed, even when call premiums were much higher than they are today, and that's precisely why it has always been difficult for option writers to earn an above average return on their investment capital when selling calls against their common stock portfolios. As I stated in Chapter 6, the sale of call options against common stocks will likely underperform the re-turn from risk-free money market instruments.

Even at today's lower premium level, however, the sale of call options can still be a major part of your investment program. But now, more than ever, the basis of a successful strategy must be the use of undervalued securities for the long side of your hedge portfolio. For investors who have been selling calls against common stock holdings and who have seen call premiums fall lower and lower, there is an alternative. It is the sale of *normally valued calls* against the purchase of *undervalued convertibles*. This strategy, which previously was an intelligent alternative for those familiar with convertibles, has become the only profitable choice for investors who wish to continue writing call options. There are excellent reasons to substitute convertibles for common stocks in an option writing program.

THE ADVANTAGES OF HEDGING WITH CONVERTIBLES

As shown by Exhibit 7–1, there are 130 convertibles having listed call options available on their underlying common stocks. From this large

Exhibit 7–1
Convertibles having listed options, February 1978

Underlying stock	Description	Underlying stock	Description
AMF, Inc.	4.250–81	Continental Oil	$2.00 pr
Aetna Life & Casualty	$2.00 pr	Continental Telephone	5.250–86
Aluminum Co. of America ..	5.250–91	Control Data	3.750–89
Amerada Hess	$3.50 pr	Deere	5.500–01
American Home Products ..	$2.00 pr	Delta Air Lines	6.500–86
American Hospital Supply ..	5.750–99	Digital Equipment	4.500–02
American Telephone		Duke Power	$6.75 pr
& Telegraph	$4.00 pr	El Paso	6.000–93
Ashland Oil	4.750–93	Engelhard Minerals	
Atlantic Richfield	$3.00 pr	& Chemicals	5.250–97
Atlantic Richfield	$2.80 pr	Federal National Mortgage ..	4.375–96
Baxter Travenol Labs	4.375–91	Flour	$3.00 pr
Baxter Travenol Labs	4.750–01	Ford Motor	4.500–96
Bristol-Myers	$2.00 pr	Ford Motor	4.875–98
Burlington Northern	$2.85 pr	GAF Corp.	$1.20 pr
Burlington Northern	5.250–92	General Telephone	
CBS, Inc.	$1.00 pr	& Electric	$2.50 pr
Carrier	$1.86 pr	General Telephone	
Carrier	5.125–89	& Electric	4.000–90
Champion International	$1.20 pr	General Telephone	
Chase Manhattan	4.875–93	& Electric	5.000–92
Chase Manhattan	6.500–96	General Telephone	
Citicorp	5.750–00	& Electric	6.250–96
City Investing	$1.31 pr	Georgia Pacific	5.250–96
City Investing	$2.00 pr	Grace, W .R.	4.250–90
City Investing	7.500–90	Grace, W .R.	6.500–96
Coastal States Gas	$1.83 pr	Greyhound	6.500–90
Coastal States Gas	$1.19 pr	Greyhound	6.000–86
Commonwealth Edison	$1.42 pr	Gulf & Western	$3.87 pr
Consolidated Edison	$6.00 pr	Gulf & Western	$2.50 pr

Exhibit 7–1 (*continued*)

Underlying stock	Description
Gulf & Western	5.500–93
Hercules	6.500–99
Heublein	4.500–97
Hilton Hotels	5.500–95
Holiday Inns	series A
Household Finance	$2.37 pr
Household Finance	$2.50 pr
International Minerals & Chemicals	4.000–91
International Telephone & Telegraph	$4.00 H
International Telephone & Telegraph	$4.50 I
International Telephone & Telegraph	$4.00 J
International Telephone & Telegraph	$4.00 K
International Telephone & Telegraph	$2.25 N
International Telephone & Telegraph	$5.00 O
International Telephone & Telegraph	8.625–00
K Mart	6.000–99
Litton Industries	Pref stk
Litton Industries	3.500–87
Lucky Stores	6.750–00
MGIC Investment	5.000–93
McDonnell Douglas	4.750–91
Minnesota Mining & Manufacturing	4.250–97
Monsanto	$2.75 pr
National Distillers & Chemicals	4.500–92
Norton Simon	$1.60 pr
Occidental Petroleum	$2.16 pr
Occidental Petroleum	$3.60 pr
Occidental Petroleum	$4.00 pr
Owens-Illinois	$4.75 pr
Owens-Illinois	4.500–92
Pennzoil	$1.33 pr
Pennzoil	5.250–96
PepsiCo	4.750–96
Pfizer	4.000–97

Underlying stock	Description
RCA Corp.	$4.00 pr
RCA Corp.	4.500–92
Ralston Purina	5.750–00
Reserve Oil & Gas	$1.75 pr
Reynolds (R. J.) Industries	$2.25 pr
Reynolds Metals	$4.50 pr
Reynolds Metals	4.500–91
Rockwell International	$4.75 pr
Rockwell International	$1.35 pr
Rockwell International	4.250–91
Searle, G. D.	5.250–89
Searle, G. D.	4.500–92
Sperry Rand	6.000–00
Sun Co.	$2.25 pr
TRW, Inc.	series 1
TRW, Inc.	series 3
Teledyne	$6.00 pr
Tenneco	6.250–92
Tenneco	$5.50 pr
Tesoro Petroleum	$2.16 pr
Tesoro Petroleum	5.250–89
Texasgulf	$3.00 pr
Travelers	$2.00 pr
UAL, Inc.	$0.40 pr
UAL, Inc.	8.000–03
UAL, Inc.	5.000–91
UAL, Inc.	4.250–92
Union Pacific	$0.47 pr
Union Pacific	4.750–99
United States Steel	5.750–01
United Technologies	$8.00 pr
United Technologies	$7.32 pr
Virginia Electric & Power	3.625–86
Walter, Jim	$1.60 pr
Walter, Jim	5.750–91
Western Union	$4.60 pr
Western Union	$4.90 pr
Western Union	5.250–97
Weyerhaeuser	$2.80 pr
Williams Companies	$0.80 pr
Woolworth	$2.20 pr
Xerox	6.000–95

Note: Some of these convertibles trade under different names than those of their underlying common stocks, and some have very complex conversion terms. Always consult a reputable service that specializes in convertible securities for specific data before making a buy or sell decision.

list, 30 or more convertibles on different stocks may usually be selected that offer significant risk/reward advantages. The March 1978 listing from *Advanced Investment Strategies*™ [1] for example, is reprinted as Exhibit 7–2 and shows 32 candidates that met careful selection parameters at that time. From this list of 32 convertibles, a diversified portfolio of hedge positions may be constructed that offers significant advantages over the conventional call writing program against common stocks.

Yield advantage. Among the 32 undervalued convertibles having listed call options from Exhibit 7–2, a full half offer a *current* yield advantage over their related common stocks. (The figure increases to two thirds if we exclude the utilities). More importantly, the convertibles, being senior securities, have a more secure yield. They will still be the better choice in those cases where no yield advantage exists. In addition, as the discounted convertible bonds approach maturity, their market price will rise to par value, providing extra capital appreciation.

Risk reduction. The very essence of an undervalued convertible is its limited risk. If an investor is aggressive (desiring the full upside participation of the market), he can achieve this objective and yet minimize the risks normally associated with stock market investing, as shown in Chapters 2 and 4. This advantage can be truly appreciated by studying the convertibles of Exhibit 7–2. If their underlying common stocks were to advance by 50 percent on average, the convertibles are expected to rise by 44 percent. On the downside, however, the convertibles are expected to drop by only 18 percent for a 50-percent decline by their underlying common stocks over the near term. The select group of 32, therefore, offers nearly 90 percent of the upside gain while cutting downside risk to less than half.

Lower commissions. Unlike most investment programs where securities are purchased for the long term and only replaced occasionally, the commission expenses for an aggressively managed hedge program can be the deciding factor as to whether or not your performance goals are achieved. *In all but one case, the convertibles of Exhibit 7–2 can be purchased at lower commission expense than their underlying common stocks.* The commissions to purchase bonds are always less than for stocks, and when the convertible preferred is at a higher price than its common, it may also be purchased at lower commissions. But even

---

[1] *Advanced Investment Strategies*™ is an investment advisory service published monthly by Thomas C. Noddings and Associates, Inc.

more important is our basic assumption that the convertibles will be held for longer periods of time than will common stocks in most option writing programs. Since the sale of normally valued calls against convertibles provides a superior risk/reward advantage to selling overpriced calls against common stock, it will not be necessary to turn over

Exhibit 7-2

						ESTIMATED CONVERTIBLE GAIN OR LOSS ASSUMING THAT STOCK PRICES CHANGE BY*	
COMPANY	CONV. DESCRIP.	NO. SHARES	APPROX. PRICES STOCK	CONV.	CONV. PREM.	+50%	−50%
Amerada Hess**	$3.50	2.20	24	55	4%	+45%	−20%
American Tel & Tel	$4.00	1.05	60	64	1	50	24
Carrier**	$1.86	1.82	16	29	0	50	24
Champion International	$1.20	1.00	17	18	6	45	24
Commonwealth Edison	$1.42	0.72	28	20	0	50	15
Consolidated Edison	$6.00	3.25	23	75	0	50	16
Deere	5.50-01	30.53	24	87	19	30	15
Duke Power	$6.75	3.91	20	83	6	40	5
El Paso	6.00-93	59.03	15	89	0	50	15
Federal Nat'l. Mtg.	4.37-96	50.95	14	71	0	50	14
Ford Motor	4.50-96	16.00	42	69	3	45	12
GAF	$1.20	1.25	11	16	16	35	5
General Tel. & Elec.	4.00-90	21.23	29	69	12	35	8
Grace (W.R.)	6.50-96	33.75	24	88	9	40	12
Greyhound	6.50-90	54.42	13	84	19	25	3
Gulf & Western	$3.87	4.82	12	58	0	50	22
Hilton Hotels	5.50-95	32.79	27	93	5	45	22
Holiday Inns	Class A	1.50	15	25	11	40	25
Household Finance	$2.37	2.25	18	40	0	50	30
ITT	$4.00K	1.56	27	48	14	30	8
Lucky Stores	6.75-00	69.01	13	100	11	35	20
National Distillers	4.50-92	39.97	21	86	2	45	21
Occidental Petroleum	$2.16	1.60	22	35	0	50	30
Owens-Illinois	4.50-92	33.90	20	80	18	30	15
Pennzoil	5.25-96	26.14	29	79	4	45	16
Rockwell Int'l.	$4.75	2.475	30	74	0	50	25
Sun Co.	$2.25	1.04	36	37	0	50	30
Tenneco	6.25-92	36.10	29	102	0	50	22
Travelers	$2.00	1.10	30	34	3	45	22
TRW	$4.40	2.20	32	72	2	50	25
United Technologies	$7.32	2.67	35	102	9	40	15
Woolworth	$2.20	1.42	18	27	6	45	5
						44	18

UNDERVALUED CONVERTIBLES HAVING LISTED CALL OPTIONS March, 1978
- Risk/reward ratio = 1.6 or higher†
- Conversion premium = 20% or less

$$\dagger\ \text{Risk/reward ratio} = \frac{50\% \text{ stock decline}}{\% \text{ convertible decline}} \times \frac{\% \text{ convertible advance}}{50\% \text{ stock advance}}$$

* Price projections are by courtesy of Value Line .
** Listed put options are also available.

NOTE: Where a company has more than one convertible, we have shown the one we believed best at the time. Before taking a position however, always evaluate other convertibles, as daily price movements may change their relative values.

the long side of the portfolio as frequently. As long as the convertibles remain undervalued, future calls that are just normally priced may be continually sold against them. Of course, if the convertible becomes overpriced, we would be happy to pay the commissions by taking the unexpected profits.

These advantages can be appreciated more fully by studying alternate strategies utilizing common stocks versus undervalued convertibles. For illustration purposes, I have chosen Amerada Hess as my example since it is one of only two undervalued convertibles that has both listed puts and calls trading. We will therefore be able to evaluate a number of different hedging strategies using the same convertible.

THE AMERADA HESS CONVERTIBLE

Exhibit 7–3 illustrates the Amerada Hess $3.50 convertible preferred. As shown, the preferred can be expected to trade on a curve at prices which are related to both its value as a straight nonconvertible preferred (estimated investment value) and its conversion value. If the common stock advances 40 percent (from $25 to $35), the preferred will rise 35 percent (from $57 to $77). If the stock falls 40 percent to $15, the convertible preferred is expected to drop only 18 percent to $47. In addition to this risk/reward advantage of nearly 2:1, the preferred yields 6.1 percent versus only 3.2 percent for the common.

The hedging strategies to follow (in this and subsequent chapters) will be based on prices for the various Amerada Hess securities that were representative of trading during February 1978. Rounded for ease of illustration, they are:

> Amerada Hess common stock = $25
> $3.50 convertible preferred   = $57
> Six-month August call option = $ 2¼
> Six-month August put option   = $ 1¾

Before evaluating the risk/reward characteristics of selling call options against the undervalued convertible of Amerada Hess, let me first analyze the conventional sale of calls against common stock. For the calculation of meaningful profit and loss estimates, appropriate income and expense items will be included. Our only exception will be commissions relating to the securities purchased for the long side of the hedge positions. For any hedging strategy to make sense, we must assume that the long side (stocks or convertibles) will be held for a reasonably long period of time.

Exhibit 7–3
Amerada Hess $3.50 convertible preferred, February 1978
(issue size, 6 million shares; converts into 2.20 shares)

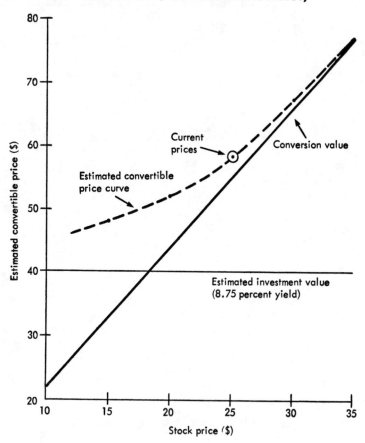

WRITING COVERED CALLS AGAINST COMMON STOCK

Exhibit 7–4 presents a detailed risk/reward analysis based on the sale of four call options at 2¼ against 400 shares of common stock at $25. The net investment of $9,150, as shown, is the value of the stock minus the net proceeds received from the sale of the calls ($10,000 − $850 = $9,150).

The risk/reward analysis of Exhibit 7–4 assumes that the stock will trade within a $15 to $35 price range at the time the calls expire in six months. The analysis also assumes that the hedge position will be held without change during that time period. If the stock is trading below $25, the calls will be allowed to expire worthless, and if the stock is trading above $25, the calls will be bought back at their intrinsic value (stock price

Exhibit 7–4
Amerada Hess—Writing covered calls against common stock, February 1978

Position
Buy 400 common stock at 25	=	$10,000
Sell 4 Aug 25 calls at 2¼	=	(900)
Commissions	=	50
Net investment	=	$ 9,150

Risk/reward analysis

Stock price at expiration	15	20	25	30	35
Call price at expiration	0	0	0	5	10
Profit or (loss)—stock	(4,000)	(2,000)	0	2,000	4,000
—calls	900	900	900	(1,100)	(3,100)
Dividends for six months	160	160	160	160	160
Commissions	(50)	(50)	(50)	(120)	(140)
Net profit or (loss)	(2,990)	(990)	1,010	940	920
Percent return—six months	−32.7	−10.8	+11.0	+10.3	+10.1
—annualized	−65.4	−21.6	+22.0	+20.6	+20.2

Probability analysis

Stock price change	Stock price	Probability		Annualized profit or loss		
+0%	$35	0.1	X	+20.2%	=	+2.02%
+20	30	0.2	X	+20.6	=	+4.12
0	25	0.4	X	+22.0	=	+8.80
−20	20	0.2	X	−21.6	=	−4.32
−40	15	0.1	X	−65.4	=	−6.54
Expected profit					=	+4.08%

minus the exercise price). Note the higher commission expenses for purchase of the in-the-money calls at stock prices of $30 and $35.

As shown by Exhibit 7–4, this covered writing strategy offers an annualized return of about 20 percent if the stock ends up at $25 or higher, while exposing one's capital to somewhat less downside risk than owning the common stock unhedged. A superficial analysis of the risk/reward calculations, as presented by most computer printouts, might indicate this covered writing strategy to be a superior investment opportunity, particularly if the large potential loss at a stock price at $15 were not considered—the loss possibly being intentionally omitted or "wished away" by someone who is bullish on the stock.

How often have you heard a stock market technician say that the stock just can't go below a certain price because the charts show large support at that price? Or a research report on the company might "prove" that the stock has nowhere to go but up. Yes, both technical and fundamental analyses are used extensively to sell the merits of a covered writing strategy like the example shown for Amerada Hess. But if someone is truly bullish on a company, why should he limit his upside opportunity by selling call options against his stock? A six-month price advance to $35 by Amerada Hess common would provide the unhedged owner of the stock an 83-percent annualized profit compared to only 20 percent for the covered call option hedge. On the other hand, if the technician or fundamentalist were bearish on Amerada Hess, there would be no reason to own the stock under any circumstances including its use in an option writing program.

The sale of call options is an important investment tool that should only be used to increase one's total return over a market cycle. Technical or fundamental opinions on the common stock should have little or no bearing as to whether or not you achieve this objective. Accordingly, call options should only be sold against common stock when premiums are abnormally high. This was not the case with Amerada Hess in February 1978. As shown by the probability analysis of Exhibit 7–4, selling call options against common stock is likely to provide an expected profit of only about 4 percent annually over the long term, less than that from risk-free money market instruments. The only individual who does well time and again with this strategy is the broker—on the commissions earned.

WRITING COVERED CALLS AGAINST CONVERTIBLES

As illustrated previously, the $3.50 convertible preferred of Amerada Hess offered substantial advantages over the common stock. The convertible offered nearly the same upside potential as the common at much less downside risk, while providing a higher yield. The preferred was obviously a far superior investment than the common stock. For those writing covered call options, how might the preferred be employed as an alternative to the common stock, and what is the expected profit?

The purchase of 200 shares of the convertible preferred is roughly comparable to 400 shares of common stock since each preferred share converts into 2.2 shares of common. Exhibit 7–5 shows a covered hedge of four call options sold at 2¼ versus 200 shares of preferred at $57. The net investment is $10,550, and we will again assume that the common stock trades within a price range of $15 to $35 over a six-month period.

As shown by Exhibit 7–5, the convertible hedge provides as much up-

Exhibit 7–5
Amerada Hess—Writing covered calls against convertibles, February 1978

Position
Buy 200 preferred stock at 57	=	$11,400
Sell 4 Aug 25 calls at 2¼	= (	900)
Commissions	=	50

Net investment   = $10,550

Risk/reward analysis

	15	20	25	30	35
Stock price at expiration	15	20	25	30	35
Call price at expiration	0	0	0	5	10
Estimated convertible price	47	51	57	67	77
Profit or (loss)—preferred	(2,000)	(1,200)	0	2,000	4,000
—calls	900	900	900	(1,100)	(3,100)
Dividends for six months	350	350	350	350	350
Commissions	(50)	(50)	(50)	(120)	(140)
Net profit or (loss)	(800)	0	1,200	1,130	1,110
Percent return—six months	− 7.6	0	+11.4	+10.7	+10.5
—annualized	−15.2	0	+22.8	+21.4	+21.0

Probability analysis

Stock price change	Stock price	Probability		Annualized profit or loss		
+40%	$35	0.1	×	+21.0%	=	+ 2.10%
+20	30	0.2	×	+21.4	=	+ 4.28
0	25	0.4	×	+22.8	=	+ 9.12
−20	20	0.2	×	0	=	0
−40	15	0.1	×	−15.2	=	− 1.52
Expected profit					=	+13.98%

side potential as the common stock hedge of Exhibit 7–4—about 20 percent annualized return at stock prices of $25 or higher. The real advantage, however, is *greater downside safety*. At a stock price of $20, the convertible hedge should break even compared to a 22-percent annualized loss for the stock hedge. At a stock price of $15, anticipated loss is only 15 percent versus 66 percent.

The downside safety of the convertible hedge translates into a much higher expected profit as demonstrated by the probability calculations of Exhibit 7–5. The convertible hedge offers a 14-percent annual return on investment compared to only 4 percent for the stock hedge.

HEDGING ON MARGIN

As demonstrated in Chapter 2, the purchase of undervalued convertibles on margin may be a prudent alternative to buying the common stock for cash. Likewise, the use of margin in a convertible/call option

Exhibit 7–6

WORK SHEET FOR EVALUATING PUT/CALL OPTION HEDGES

COMPANY _Amerada Hess_

DATE _February 1978_

DESCRIPTION OF SECURITIES

Convertible _$3.50 preferred_   Interest or Dividend Dates _Jan, Apr, Jul, Oct_

	Exer. Price	Expir. Month	Symbol	Value Line Rank	Value Line Volatility	Target Prices	Current Yield
Common Stock			AHC	4	110	25	3.2%
Convertible			AHC Pr	3	90	57	6.1
Put option							
Call option	25	Aug	HE				

Conversion value = _2.20_ shares x $ _25.00_ per share = $ _55.00_

Premium over conversion value = _3.6_ %

Estimated investment value (per Value Line) = $ _40.00_

Premium over investment value = _42.5_ %

POSSIBLE HEDGE POSITION: Bullish _✓_,   Neutral _____,   Bearish _____

Common stock:	_____ at $ _____ = $ _____ + _____ comm.				= $ _____
Convertibles:	_200_ at $ _57_ = $ _11400_ + _160_ comm.				= $ _11560_
Puts bought:	_____ at $ _____ = $ _____ + _____ comm.				= $ +
Calls sold:	_4_ at $ _225_ = $ _900_ – _55_ comm.				= – _845_
Net investment:	unleveraged				= $ _10715_
	leveraged (_50% x 11560 – 845_)				= $ _4935_

ESTIMATED PROFIT OR LOSS AT EXPIRATION DATE: unleveraged _____, leveraged _✓_

	Downside	Exercise Price(s)		Upside
Assumed stock price	_15_	_25_	_30_	_35_
Est. convertible price	_47_	_57_	_67_	_77_
Est. put price				
Est. call price	_0_	_0_	_5_	_10_
Profit or (loss) - stock .... (_____)				
- conv .... (_2000_)		_0_	_2000_	_4000_
- puts				
- calls	_900_	_900_	(_1100_)	(_3100_)
Income received	_350_	_350_	_350_	_350_
Margin interest at _8.0_ % .... (	_230_) (	_230_) (	_230_) (	_230_)
Commissions .... (	_55_) (	_55_) (	_120_) (	_140_)
Estimated gain or (loss)	_1035_	_965_	_900_	_880_
Estimated return on investment	– _21.0%_	+ _19.6%_	+ _18.2%_	+ _17.8_ %
Annualized ROI (_.50_ years)	– _42.0%_	+ _39.2%_	+ _36.4%_	+ _35.6_ %

hedge may also be more conservative than writing calls against common stock on a nonmargined basis.

Exhibit 7–6 provides a detailed worksheet analysis of the covered calls sold against Amerada Hess convertibles from Exhibit 7–5. As shown, the use of margin increases the upside potential of the hedge to well above 30 percent annualized, while still maintaining a lower risk posture than the nonmargined common stock hedge of Exhibit 7–4. The two positions are graphically compared by Exhibit 7–7.

Exhibit 7–7
Alternate hedges in Amerada Hess, February 1978

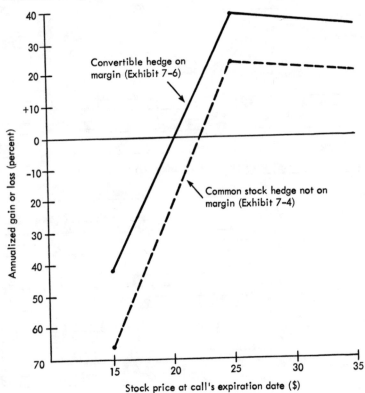

In addition to helping one analyze risks as well as rewards, the use of a standard worksheet, like Exhibit 7–6, helps to minimize errors when evaluating hedge positions. The analysis requires one to include also all cost factors such as margin interest and appropriate commissions. Accordingly, a worksheet of this type should always be employed before ever taking a hedge position.

WRITING CALL OPTIONS IN VARIABLE RATIOS

One of the most successful investment strategies in recent years has been the sale of call options in ratios greater than 1:1, especially when call premiums were higher. Since the variable (ratio) hedge involves the combination of covered and *naked* calls, the strategy has received only limited recognition by the financial press because most institutional investors are prevented by law from selling naked options regardless of the risk/reward probabilities. And many brokerage firms discourage their sale for all but their largest, most sophisticated clients.

The prevailing Wall Street position is that selling covered calls is conservative, but selling naked calls is speculative. How silly can they get? Is it more risky to sell 11 calls against 1,000 shares of AT&T (or whatever stock) instead of 10? Or, how about selling 12 calls or 15, or 20? When calls are trading out-of-the-money, is the sale of a low-priced covered call more conservative than a ratio hedge? I could go on, but why bother. As with most superior investment strategies, the best tactic will normally be that which is counter to the simplistic "wisdom" of Wall Street or La Salle Street.

Exhibits 7–8 and 7–9 present 3:1 ratio hedges using six-month Amerada Hess $30 call options sold against common stock and the convertible preferred respectively. As shown, the ratio hedges provide about the same downside protection as the covered hedges of Exhibits 7–4 and 7–5. So, by that standard they are no more risky than the covered hedges using $25 options. Accordingly, the extra risk must lie on the upside. But how does one define risk? Exhibit 7–8, for example, shows that the ratio hedge offers a 65-percent annualized rate of return at a price of $30 compared to only a 20-percent annual return on investment for the covered hedge against common stock per Exhibit 7–4. The extra risk obviously comes in if the stock were to advance well above $30. At a price of $35, for instance, the ratio hedge would show a loss as compared to the profit for the covered hedge. But what are the odds of this happening, and couldn't one close out his total position if the stock were to advance quickly toward $35? On the way up, the $30 call option would probably sell for no more than 2 when the stock reached $30, even if it still had a few months to run. At prices of $30 for the stock and 2 for the option, the total position could be closed out at about break-even after commissions.

So, where is the upside risk? The risk, of course, is the remote possibility that the stock would run up so fast that the position could not be

Exhibit 7–8
Amerada Hess—Ratio call writing against common stock

Position
  Buy 400 common stock at 25   = $10,000
  Sell 12 Aug 30 calls at ¾   = (900)
  Commissions   =   80
  Net investment   = $ 9,180

Risk/reward analysis

Stock price at expiration	15	20	25	30	35
Call price at expiration	0	0	0	0	5
Profit or (loss)—stock	(4,000)	(2,000)	0	2,000	4,000
—calls	900	900	900	900	(5,100)
Dividends for six months	160	160	160	160	160
Commissions	(80)	(80)	(80)	(80)	(240)
Net profit or (loss)	(3,020)	(1,020)	980	2,980	(1,180)
Percent return—six months	−32.9	−11.1	+10.7	+32.5	+12.8
—annualized	−65.8	−22.2	+21.4	+65.0	−25.6

Probability analysis

Stock price change	Stock price	Probability		Annualized profit or loss		
+40%	$35	0.1	×	−25.6%	=	− 2.56%
+20	30	0.2	×	+65.0	=	+13.00
0	25	0.4	×	+21.4	=	+ 8.56
−20	20	0.2	×	−22.2	=	− 4.44
−40	15	0.1	×	−65.8	=	− 6.58
Expected profit					=	+ 7.98%

closed out in time to avoid a loss, as in a tender offer. From a practical standpoint, however, this will happen so infrequently that the extra profits realized from other ratio hedges in a diversified portfolio will more than offset these occasional upside losses.

My experience conclusively demonstrates (to my satisfaction anyway) that covered option writers will experience far more losing positions in a bear market than will those employing ratio hedges in a bull market. And the losses for the covered positions will generally be larger. I must therefore conclude that carefully selected and managed ratio hedges are more prudent than is covered call writing.

The probability calculations of Exhibits 7–8 and 7–9 confirm that the ratio hedges offer greater opportunity for profit than do the covered hedges of Exhibits 7–4 and 7–5. But be extra careful when selling low-priced, out-of-the-money options. An eighth or a quarter of a point can mean the difference between profit and loss. If the $30 calls were sold

Exhibit 7–9
Amerada Hess—Ratio call writing against convertibles

Position
Buy 200 preferred stock at 57 = $11,400
Sell 12 Aug calls at ¾ = (900)
Commissions = 80
Net investment = $10,580

Risk/reward analysis

Stock price at expiration	15	20	25	30	35
Call price at expiration	0	0	0	0	5
Estimated convertible price	47	51	57	67	77
Profit or (loss)—preferred	(2,000)	(1,200)	0	2,000	4,000
—calls	900	900	900	900	(5,100)
Dividends for six months	350	350	350	350	350
Commissions	(80)	(80)	(80)	(80)	(240)
Net profit or (loss)	(830)	(30)	1,170	3,170	(990)
Percent return—six months	− 7.8	−0.3	+11.1	+30.0	− 9.4
—annualized	−15.6	−0.6	+22.2	+60.0	−18.8

Probability analysis

Stock price change	Stock price	Probability		Annualized profit or loss		
+40%	$35	0.1	X	−18.8%	=	− 1.88%
+20	30	0.2	X	+60.0	=	+12.00
0	25	0.4	X	+22.2	=	+ 8.88
−20	20	0.2	X	− 0.6	=	− 0.12
−40	15	0.1	X	−15.6	=	− 1.56
Expected profit					=	+17.32%

for ½ instead of ¾ as used in the calculations, for example, the expected profit for the stock/call hedge of Exhibit 7–8 would be reduced from 8 percent to less than 2 percent. So, in addition to employing worksheets for analyzing hedge positions, you should also calculate the expected profit that the position offers.

Exhibit 7–10 illustrates a worksheet analysis of the ratio hedge against convertibles on full margin. Note that when calls are sold to hedge convertibles, the number of calls which are considered covered for margin purposes correspond to the largest round lot of shares obtainable through conversion. All the rest are considered uncovered (or naked) and must be margined as such. Each share of the Amerada Hess preferred converts into 2.2 shares of common, so the 200 preferred represent an equivalent of 440 shares of common stock. In this case, four of the twelve calls are covered, and eight are naked (requiring additional collateral of $2,000).

Exhibit 7–10

WORK SHEET FOR EVALUATING PUT/CALL OPTION HEDGES

COMPANY *Amerada Hess*   DATE *February 1978*

DESCRIPTION OF SECURITIES

Convertible *$3.50 preferred*   Interest or Dividend Dates *Jan, Apr, Jul, Oct*

	Exer. Price	Expir. Month	Symbol	Value Line Rank	Value Line Volatility	Target Prices	Current Yield
Common Stock			*AHC*	*4*	*110*	*25*	*3.2%*
Convertible			*AHC Pr*	*3*	*90*	*57*	*6.1*
Put option							
Call option	*30*	*Aug*	*HF*				

Conversion value = _*2.20*_ shares x $ _*25.00*_ per share = $ _*55.00*_
Premium over conversion value   = _*3.6*_ %
Estimated investment value (per Value Line)   = $ _*40.00*_
Premium over investment value   = _*42.5*_ %

POSSIBLE HEDGE POSITION: Bullish _____,   Neutral _✓_,   Bearish _____

Common stock:	___ at $ ___ = $ ___	+ ___ comm.	= $ ___
Convertibles:	*200* at $ *57* = $ *11400*	+ *160* comm.	= $ *11560*
Puts bought:	___ at $ ___ = $ ___	+ ___ comm.	= + ___
Calls sold:	*12* at $ *75* = $ *900*	− *80* comm.	= − *820*
Net investment:	unleveraged		= $ *10740*
	leveraged (_*50% x 11560 + 8 x 250−820*_)		= $ *6960*

ESTIMATED PROFIT OR LOSS AT EXPIRATION DATE: unleveraged _____, leveraged _✓_

	Downside	Exercise Price(s)		Upside
Assumed stock price	*15*	*25*	*30*	*35*
Est. convertible price	*47*	*57*	*67*	*77*
Est. put price				
Est. call price	*0*	*0*	*0*	*5*
Profit or (loss) - stock ....(	*2000*)	*0*	*2000*	*4000*
- conv ....(	*2000*)	*0*	*2000*	*4000*
- puts	*900*	*900*	*900*	(*5100*)
- calls	*900*	*900*	*900*	(*5100*)
Income received......................	*350*	*350*	*350*	*350*
Margin interest at _*8.0*_ % ....(	*150*) (	*150*) (	*150*) (	*150*)
Commissions ....(	*80*) (	*80*) (	*80*) (	*240*)
Estimated gain or (loss) ....(	*980*)	*1020*	*3020*	(*1140*)
Estimated return on investment	− *14.1*%	+ *14.7*%	+ *43.4*%	− *16.4* %
Annualized ROI (_.50_ years)	− *28.2*%	+ *29.4*%	+ *86.8* %	− *32.8*%

In summary:

1. Call writing against common stock is no longer a winning strategy since premiums are just too low.
2. Call writing against convertibles is still a profitable strategy when carefully selected.
3. Downside break-even limits do not describe either the *real risk* of common/option hedges or the *real safety* of convertible/option hedges.
4. The use of margin is prudent if employed in a convertible hedge strategy offering a high expected profit at low risk.
5. Carefully selected and managed ratio hedges are more prudent than covered writing.

8

AN ULTRACONSERVATIVE
HEDGING STRATEGY

The previous chapter demonstrated how the sale of listed call options against undervalued convertibles can offer upside potential at a lower risk posture than most investment strategies. But since the list of convertible securities having listed options represents only a small portion of the total convertible market, how can the hedger take advantage of other undervalued opportunities?

The answer is selling common stock short against convertibles, a strategy successfully employed by serious investors long before the arrival of listed call options. In fact, this strategy is even *safer* than selling calls against convertibles, but again, it is not one widely recognized by the investment community. Most institutional money managers, for instance, are prevented by law from shorting stock, even when the short sale is made against a related convertible security. Their loss is our gain.

The following guidelines should be carefully applied when selecting convertible hedge candidates.

1. The convertible (bond or preferred) should be trading close to its conversion value. It will therefore offer nearly as much upside potential as its common stock.

2. The convertible should not be selling too far above its investment value so as to limit its decline upon a drop in price by the stock.

3. The common stock should pay little or no dividends since the hedger is obligated to pay any dividends on stock he sells short. The hedge position of long convertibles versus short stock should provide a positive cash flow to the hedger.

4. The common stock should have a history of high price volatility to improve the chances for a major price move, but the company should not be a potential bankruptcy candidate.

The strategy is ideally suited for grossly undervalued convertibles on speculative stocks that do not enjoy an institutional following. The conservative investor who will not normally consider owning a low-quality convertible can take advantage of its undervaluation by this low-risk hedging technique.

The Amerada Hess preferred, used as our example for the call option strategies in Chapter 7, is not a perfect candidate for this strategy as the stock pays a dividend and does not have the high price volatility that we would like to see. For comparison purposes with other strategies using Amerada Hess, however, let us analyze a possible convertible/common stock hedge position.

HEDGING THE AMERADA HESS CONVERTIBLE PREFERRED

Exhibit 8–1 presents a bullish hedge position involving the short sale of 200 shares of common stock against 200 preferred (representing 440 common). The 200 shares of stock were selected to give us an approximate break-even position on the downside while offering satisfactory upside profits. Alternate positions of 300 or 400 shares sold short would be considered for neutral or bearish postures.

As shown by the probability analysis of Exhibit 8–1, this hedge position offers an expected profit on our investment of 7.6 percent, or just a little more than that available from risk-free money market instruments. We would therefore search elsewhere for better opportunities. If, however, the common stock did not pay a dividend, the expected profit would be more than 10 percent, and Amerada Hess would have been an acceptable candidate.

A far better hedge candidate was the LTV convertible bond illustrated in Chapter 2. Here we had a grossly undervalued convertible combined with its nondividend-paying common stock having high price volatility. The material to follow was adapted from *How the Experts Beat the Market,* as the techniques shown in that book, for the LTV hedge in 1975 are fully applicable for today's market.

Exhibit 8–1
Amerada Hess—Selling stock short against convertibles, February 1978

Position
Buy 200 preferred stock at 57 = $11,400
Sell short 200 common at 25 =   *
Commissions (stock only) =   90
Net investment = $11,490

Risk/reward analysis

Stock price in six months	15	20	25	30	35
Estimated convertible price	47	51	57	67	77
Profit or (loss)—preferred	(2,000)	(1,200)	0	2,000	4,000
—common	2,000	1,000	0	(1,000)	(2,000)
Dividends received for six months	350	350	350	350	350
Dividends paid for six months	(160)	(160)	(160)	(160)	(160)
Stock commissions round trip	(160)	(170)	†	(200)	(210)
Net profit or (loss)	30	(180)	190	990	1,980
Percent return—six months	+0.2	−1.6	+1.6	+ 8.6	+17.2
—annualized	+0.4	−3.2	+3.2	+17.2	+34.4

Probability analysis

Stock price change	Stock price	Probability		Annualized profit or loss		
+40%	$35	0.1	×	+34.4%	=	+3.44%
+20	30	0.2	×	+17.2	=	+3.44
0	25	0.4	×	+ 3.2	=	+1.28
−20	20	0.2	×	− 3.2	=	−0.64
−40	15	0.1	×	+ 0.4	=	+0.04
Expected profit					=	+7.56%

* No funds are required for the short sale.
† Commissions are excluded as we assume that the position would be held for a major price move.

HEDGING LTV CONVERTIBLE BONDS

Let us look at the LTV 7½s of '77 convertible, as of January 1975, for hedging opportunities (Exhibit 2–3 of Chapter 2). Since the bond was trading at only a 5-percent conversion premium and its volatile common stock paid no dividend, it was a prime candidate for hedging. A step-by-step evaluation proceeded as follows:

1. **Yield advantage.** A current yield of 7½ percent was received by the bondholder, whereas the stock paid no dividend.

2. **Upside potential.** The bond had to advance almost as fast as its common stock since it was selling near conversion value. If LTV com-

mon were to double from $10 up to $20, the bond would have to advance 90 percent to its conversion value of 190 (95 shares × $20 = $1,900).

3. **Downside risk.** The bond would have declined less than the common due to the support provided by its investment floor. As shown by Exhibit 2–3 of Chapter 2, the estimated investment value was 75 and we expected a drop of only 20 percent, from 100 down to 80, if the stock declined by 50 percent to $5.

4. **Mathematical advantage.** Assuming that LTV common either doubled or dropped in half (equal probabilities), the convertible bond's mathematical advantage (or risk/reward ratio) was calculated as follows:

$$MA = \frac{\text{Percent convertible advance}}{\text{100 percent stock advance}} \times \frac{\text{50 percent stock decline}}{\text{Percent convertible decline}}$$

$$= \frac{90}{100} \times \frac{50}{20} = 2.2$$

The risk/reward ratio of 2.2 for the LTV bond was exceptionally high and was even greater if the 7½ percent bond yield was included in the calculation.

Note that I chose price moves by LTV common stock of −50% and +100% since these represented equal probabilities for future price action assuming no price bias or fixed time frame. If a stock drops in half, it must later double in price to get back to the starting price; or if it first doubles, a 50-percent decline would also bring it back to the starting price. Other equal probability combinations could also have been considered, e.g., −20/+25 or −33/+50, but a major move is generally needed to close out a hedge position of this type with significant profits after commission expenses.

Note also that an equal probability combination like −50/+100 is independent of the length of time the position is held. It might, for example, take several years for a stock to experience this large a move. When we assume a short time frame as when selling six-month call options, I believe that equal percentage moves like −25/+25 are more appropriate. This recognizes the fact that stocks tend to decline more rapidly in bear markets than they advance in bull markets.

5. **Alternate hedge positions.** Depending on your personal investment goals, desired risk posture, and other securities in your portfolio, a convertible hedge in LTV could have been designed to meet a number

of different objectives. By definition, the three common types of convertible hedges are:

Bullish hedge—upside profits at downside break-even.

Neutral hedge—modest profits in any kind of market.

Bearish hedge—downside profits at upside break-even.

Bullish and bearish hedges in LTV are shown in Exhibit 8–2, a neutral hedge would fall between these two extremes.

Exhibit 8–2
Alternate hedge positions in LTV convertible bonds (investment = 10 bonds × $1,000 = $10,000)

	Stock price move	
	−50%	+100%
Bullish hedge		
Stock sold short = 400 shares × $10 = $4,000		
Downside risk		
Profit on stock sold short = $ 4,000 × 50%	$2,000	
Loss on bonds purchased = $10,000 × 20%	(2,000)	
Upside potential		
Profit on bonds purchased = $10,000 × 90%		$9,000
Loss on stock sold short = $ 4,000 × 100%		(4,000)
Net profit or (loss)	$ 0	$5,000
Return on investment	0%	+50%
Bearish hedge		
Stock sold short = 900 shares × $10 = $9,000		
Downside potential		
Profit on stock sold short = $ 9,000 × 50%	$4,500	
Loss on bonds purchased = $10,000 × 20%	(2,000)	
Upside risk		
Profit on bonds purchased = $10,000 × 90%		$9,000
Loss on stock sold short = $ 9,000 × 100%		(9,000)
Net profit or (loss)	$2,500	$ 0
Return on investment	+25%	0%

Note: Bond interest and commissions were excluded from the above calculations for simplification.

6. **Selecting the best hedge ratio.** How to select the best hedge ratio has been the most frequently raised question during my entire investment career. As illustrated by Exhibit 8–2, a bullish hedge provides greater profit potential during the upside phase of a market cycle than a bearish hedge does during the downside phase. Convertible hedgers who do not exercise market judgment should therefore favor a bullish posture since it will produce optimum profits over a market cycle. On the other hand, some investors will employ bearish hedges based on their market outlook or to protect other unhedged holdings against a

market crash. Bearish hedges frequently provide cash flows competitive with money market instruments while still offering substantial profits during stock market declines. The choice is yours.

CONVERTIBLE/STOCK HEDGE WORKSHEETS

Exhibit 8–3 illustrates the use of a standard worksheet for evaluating convertible/stock hedges by using the bullish hedge in LTV as the example and assuming a 12-month position.

Exhibit 8–3

WORKSHEET FOR EVALUATING CONVERTIBLE HEDGES

COMPANY _____*LTV*_____   DATE _*Jan. '75*_

DESCRIPTION OF SECURITIES

Description	Symbol	Target Prices	Current Yield
Common stock.........	*LTV*	*10*	*0* %
Convertible.......... *7½ -77*		*100*	*7.5*

Conversion value = _*95.24*_ shares x $ _*10.00*_ = $ _*952*_
Conversion premium   = _*5*_ %
Estimated investment value   = $ _*750*_

	1972	1973	1974
Stock price ranges	*9- 14¾*	*7½ -13½*	*7⅞ -12½*

POSSIBLE HEDGE POSITION: Bullish _✓_, Neutral _____, or Bearish_____

Convertibles purchased: _*10 M*_ at $ *1,000* each = $ _*10,000*_
Stock sold short: *400* shs. at $ *10.00* each = $ _*4,000*_
Investment = $*10,000*+ $ _*150*_ commission = $ _*10,150*_

PROFIT OR LOSS ESTIMATES – ASSUMING A 12–MONTH POSITION (unleveraged))

	-50%	0%	+50%	+100%
Assumed stock price change				
Stock price	*5*	*10*	*15*	*20*
Estimated convertible price	*80*	*100*	*143*	*190*
Profit or (loss) - convertible	(*2,000*)	*0*	*4,300*	*9,000*
- stock	*2,000*	*0*	(*2,000*)	(*4,000*)
Commissions	(*270*)	(*300*)	(*320*)	(*340*)
Estimated capital gain or (loss)...	(*270*)	(*300*)	*1,980*	*4,660*
Estimated return on investment ...	*– 2.7*%	*– 3.0* %	*+19.5*%	*+45.9*%
Income received less dividends paid on stock sold short	*+ 7.4*%	*+ 7.4* %	*+ 7.4* %	*+ 7.4* %
Net return	*+ 4.7* %	*+ 4.4* %	*+26.9*%	*+53.3*%

MARGINING CONVERTIBLE/STOCK HEDGES

As with the sale of call options against undervalued convertibles on margin, convertible/stock hedges like LTV should also be placed on margin to leverage their potential profits. Margin calculations may be included in the worksheet calculations, or you may use Exhibit 8–4 to adjust the nonmargined profit and loss estimates. Exhibit 8–4 provides convenient tables for different margin rates and different margin interest charges.

Exhibit 8–4
Factors for adjusting profit and loss estimates when using margin

	Margin rate (percent)										
	30	35	40	45	50	55	60	65	70	75	80
Profit or loss multiplier	3.33	2.86	2.50	2.22	2.00	1.82	1.67	1.54	1.43	1.33	1.25
Deduction for margin interest (percent)											
6	14.0	11.1	9.0	7.3	6.0	4.9	4.0	3.2	2.6	2.0	1.5
7	16.3	13.0	10.5	8.6	7.0	5.7	4.7	3.8	3.0	2.3	1.8
8	18.7	14.9	12.0	9.8	8.0	6.5	5.3	4.3	3.4	2.7	2.0
9	21.0	16.7	13.5	11.0	9.0	7.4	6.0	4.8	3.8	3.0	2.2
10	23.3	18.6	15.0	12.2	10.0	8.2	6.7	5.4	4.3	3.3	2.5
11	25.7	20.4	16.5	13.5	11.0	9.0	7.3	5.9	4.7	3.7	2.8
12	28.0	22.3	18.0	14.7	12.0	9.8	8.0	6.5	5.2	4.0	3.0

Examples: A specific situation is expected to provide an annual return of 15 percent including income and capital gains. It may be margined at 50 percent and current margin interest is 10 percent.

$$\text{Net return} = 2.0(15.0) - 10.0 = 30.0 - 10.0 = 20.0\%$$

A diversified portfolio is expected to provide an annual return of 14 percent. The total portfolio may be margined at 70 percent and current margin interest is 8 percent.

$$\text{Net return} = 1.43(14.0) - 3.4 = 20.0 - 3.4 = 16.6\%$$

You should first study the examples provided by Exhibit 8–4. Next, to show the results of a margined investment, we may adjust the figures for the LTV hedge from Exhibit 8–3 as follows:

Profit or loss multiplier = 2.00 based on a 50-percent margin rate.
Deduction for margin interest = 10.0 based on 10 percent interest rates prevailing in January 1975.

	Stock price change			
	−50%	0%	+50%	+100%
Net return from Exhibit 8–3	+ 4.7%	+ 4.4%	+26.9%	+ 53.3%
Times profit or loss multiplier	× 2.0	× 2.0	× 2.0	× 2.0
	+ 9.4%	+ 8.8%	+53.8%	+106.6%
Minus deduction for margin interest	−10.0	−10.0	−10.0	− 10.0
Estimated net return on full margin	− 0.6%	− 1.2%	+43.8%	+ 96.6%

Exhibit 8–5 graphically compares the leveraged hedge position with a cash purchase of LTV common stock, including commissions and interest and assuming a 12-month workout. As shown, the margined hedge position offered *the same upside potential as LTV common at little or no downside risk!*

Exhibit 8–5
The LTV convertible/stock hedge on margin

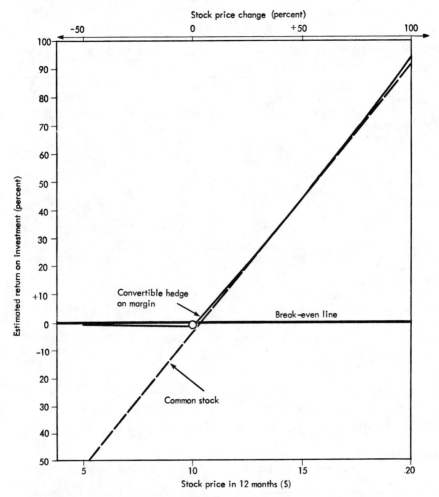

CLOSING OUT A CONVERTIBLE HEDGE ON THE UPSIDE

Convertible hedgers have a choice as to how they can close out their positions if hedges appreciate in value. They could, of course, simply sell the convertibles and purchase stock to cover the short sales. However, if the convertibles were selling at their conversion value, as would be expected after a major advance, they might consider converting a sufficient number of convertibles and covering the short position with the shares received. This maneuver would save much of the expense of close-out brokerage commissions. In this event, the hedger should make sure that the bond interest was just recently paid, since the interest accrued from the previous payment date would be lost upon conversion. This interest loss might exceed commission savings.

Income tax considerations might also favor close-out by sale instead of conversion. Let us evaluate the tax consequences for the LTV hedge from Exhibit 8–3, assuming that the stock doubled after a holding period in excess of one year (commissions are excluded).

Close-out by conversion. Those bonds converted for covering the 400 shares of stock sold short would be treated as being sold the day the stock was shorted for an approximate break-even, short-term trade. The remaining bonds would provide a long-term capital gain of about $5,000.

Close-out by sale. A long-term capital gain of $9,000 would be received on the convertible bonds versus a short-term loss of $4,000 on the stock sold short (all short sales are short-term gain or loss regardless of the time held). This result would be most advantageous if short-term gains on other transactions were taken during the year.

MANAGING CONVERTIBLE HEDGE PORTFOLIOS

Once convertible hedge portfolios are established, hedgers may simply sit back and wait for major price moves before closing positions. Or, they may monitor their portfolios continually for profit opportunities. Aggressive management of a relatively passive hedge portfolio should increase overall investment performance. Management strategies for bullish hedges include:

1. Close out a position for profit if the convertible becomes normally valued, even if the stock has not changed much. There will probably be better opportunities elsewhere for reinvesting the funds.

2. Do not wait for the stock to "double" before taking upside profits. Once the convertible has advanced much above par, the possibility of additional upside profit is offset by the other possibility that paper gains will be given back if the stock retreats.

3. Be prepared to close out positions on the downside even if the

close-out will result in a modest loss. There will probably be another opportunity available which will produce profits during the next market advance while the old hedge is simply returning to its starting point.

4. The short side of the hedge may be traded against the long side by shorting more stock during market rallies and covering stock on market dips. These adjustments will produce greater profits during sideways market movements at the expense of reduced profits if the stock were to make a sustained price advance.

Exhibit 8–6 provides guidelines for selecting and managing a convertible hedge portfolio.

Exhibit 8–6
General guides for hedging convertibles

1. Buy convertibles that are significantly undervalued—a mathematical advantage over their underlying common stocks of 2.0 or higher, including yields on both securities. The convertible should be selling close to its conversion value and not too far above its investment floor.

2. Select convertibles on common stocks that pay little or no dividends— the short seller must pay these dividends. The common stock should also have a history of high-price volatility to improve the chances for a major price move.

3. Make sure from your stockbroker that the stock is available for short selling and that there is a reasonable probability that it can be held short for as long as desired.

4. Be certain that both the convertible and stock are actively traded to permit establishing positions at favorable prices.

5. Select the amount of common stock sold short versus convertibles purchased to meet your specific investment objectives.

6. Employ margin for convertible hedges to obtain the additional leverage.

7. Close out the position if the convertible becomes overpriced, or even normally valued—the funds should be employed in another situation having more favorable risk/reward characteristics.

8. Consider closing out the position on the upside by converting the required number of convertibles to save on commission expenses—unless interest lost or tax considerations favor close-out by sale. The time required for the conversion process may also favor close-out by sale as your capital might be tied up several weeks earning nothing.

9. Avoid companies that are takeover candidates unless the convertible may be purchased at little or no conversion premium—a cash tender offer might reduce the upside potential for the convertible as it will immediately go to conversion value.

10. Avoid hedges in companies that are possible bankruptcy candidates unless you plan to establish a full bear hedge position.

9

LOW-RISK HEDGING
TACTICS UTILIZING
LISTED PUT OPTIONS

Like listed call options, listed puts offer a variety of complex strategies that most investors simply do not seem to comprehend. Here are the most flagrant examples of common nonsense that I have observed regarding this new investment tool.

FACTS AND FANTASIES OF LISTED PUT OPTIONS

Fantasy No. 1.　The purchase of put options to protect your common stocks against a market decline is like buying insurance and is a prudent tactic for conservative investors.

Facts.　This is the most commonly recommended put option strategy and is supposedly employed by investors who are uncertain about the future direction of the market. The objective is to limit downside risk to the extent of the premiums paid for the puts, while providing full upside potential (minus the put premiums, of course). *The fact that you also lose most of the premiums during a sideways market is seldom mentioned.*

Since losses are virtually assured under most probable stock market movements (down, sideways or modestly higher), I doubt that the occasional bull market will produce sufficient profits to offset the cost of this "insurance," let alone make a reasonable profit. As for being prudent, the risk/reward posture is essentially the same as for the *speculative purchase of call options.*

Fantasy No. 2.   Buy puts for bear market profits.

Facts.   I cannot argue with this strategy providing the investor is *certain* of a bear market trend and *providing he has also liquidated all of his common stock holdings.* But most investors who have "fallen in love" with their stocks will simply ride the market down, and the profits earned from the few puts that they may purchase will seldom offset their stock losses. Remember, before a put option becomes profitable, the underlying common stock must drop 5 to 10 percent over a limited period of time.

Fantasy No. 3.   Selling naked puts is a superb bull market strategy.

Facts.   The sale of naked put options, against cash as your collateral, is comparable to writing covered calls against common stock—a losing strategy at today's premium levels as I stressed in Chapter 6. If anyone is really sure that the market is heading higher over the near term, there are *far* better strategies to take advantage of this foresight.

Fantasy No. 4.   The combined purchase of a put option and the sale of a call against common stock is a conservative technique for gaining additional stock market profits.

Facts.   This strategy will seldom offer an above average performance. Yes, it's conservative, but it usually offers little or no profit. A long put versus a short call is like selling stock short. If done in combination with the purchase of stock, you have simply created a "short against the box" type position—*no risk, but no profit—except for your stockbroker!* And don't be fooled by a mix of different exercise prices and/or expiration months—the net result will almost always be a lower expected profit than from risk-free treasury bills.

HOW SHOULD THE SOPHISTICATED INVESTOR EMPLOY PUT OPTIONS?

Since all the basic put option strategies (as shown in Exhibit 5–2 of Chapter 5) are related to the underlying common stock, and since we know there are superior alternatives to stocks, how might we effectively employ put options in our overall investment program?

The most important use of puts is to purchase them for downside protection of a portfolio of convertible bonds or preferreds—especially when premiums are low. Or a typical convertible hedger may sell calls when premiums are high and buy puts when premiums are low—or use both instruments when premiums are normal, as I believe they are today.

Unfortunately, however, the present list of 25 available put options limits our ability to use them directly with undervalued convertibles. As shown by Exhibit 7–2, only Amerada Hess and Carrier have undervalued convertibles along with listed put options. But in anticipation of expanded put trading in the future, I will evaluate alternative strategies using the different securities for Amerada Hess. In later chapters, I will introduce SUPERHEDGES™ V and VI, sophisticated bear market strategies involving the extensive use of put options.

BUYING PUT OPTIONS TO "PROTECT" COMMON STOCK

Before illustrating the risk/reward characteristics of put options combined with undervalued convertibles, let us first establish a reference point by analyzing their use with common stock. I will again use Amerada Hess as the example with the common stock at $25 and six-month put options trading at 1¾.

Exhibit 9–1 provides a detailed analysis of this strategy employing 400 shares of common and 4 put options. As with previous examples, option commissions are included but stock commissions are not. As shown by

Exhibit 9–1
Amerada Hess—Common stock combined with puts

Position
Buy 400 common stock at 25	=	$10,000
Buy 4 Aug 25 puts at 1¾	=	700
Commissions	=	50
Net investment	=	$10,750

Risk/reward analysis

	15	20	25	30	35
Stock price at expiration	15	20	25	30	35
Put price at expiration	10	5	0	0	0
Profit or (loss)—stock	(4,000)	(2,000)	0	2,000	4,000
—puts	3,300	1,300	(700)	(700)	(700)
Dividends for six months	160	160	160	160	160
Commissions	(140)	(120)	(50)	(50)	(50)
Net profit or (loss)	(680)	(660)	(590)	1,410	3,410
Percent return—six months	− 6.3	− 6.1	− 5.5	+13.1	+31.7
—annualized	−12.6	−12.2	−11.0	+26.2	+63.4

Probability analysis

Stock price change	Stock price	Probability		Annualized profit or loss		
+40%	$35	0.1	×	+63.4%	=	+6.34%
+20	30	0.2	×	+26.2	=	+5.24
0	25	0.4	×	−11.0	=	−4.40
−20	20	0.2	×	−12.2	=	−2.44
−40	15	0.1	×	−12.6	=	−1.26
Expected profit					=	+3.48%

the outcomes at various stock prices, this is obviously a very bullish strategy. The common stock must make a significant price advance before a satisfactory return on investment is earned. Downside risk is limited, but that same risk is also experienced during a sideways market —the most common occurrence from a probability standpoint. The risk/ reward characteristics for this strategy therefore are comparable to the *speculative* purchase of call options, and it cannot be recommended for use by the serious investor.

The probability analysis of Exhibit 9–1 also shows that the strategy is likely to underperform short-term money market instruments, and this excludes commissions to purchase and sell the common stock. If the long side of the portfolio were turned over annually, for example, the expected profit would be nil. Yet, certain stockbrokers recommend this strategy to their "conservative" clients with every intention of turning over the common stock. The reasons are obvious. The strategy sounds conservative when sold as "insurance" and produces more than four times the commissions than for outright purchases of call options.

BUYING PUT OPTIONS TO PROTECT CONVERTIBLES

Here we have a strategy that makes good sense and it *should* be considered by serious investors. Exhibit 9–2 presents three alternatives using 200 shares of the Amerada Hess $3.50 convertible preferred (representing 440 shares of underlying common stock).

Because the convertible is inherently less risky than the common, the purchase of only two put options provides a nearly break-even downside while offering an exceptionally high profit opportunity on the upside. The higher dividends paid on the preferred plus the lower cost for only two puts also avoids the negative cash flow in a sideways market as would be experienced with the common stock hedge (Exhibit 9–1).

The purchase of additional puts (3 or 4 versus 200 preferred) shifts some of the upside potential to the downside while modestly increasing the loss in a narrow sideways market. All the alternatives shown, ranging from bullish to neutral, offer satisfactory expected profits of about 12 percent; nearly 9 percentage points higher than when using the common stock.

The best choice of the three alternatives will depend on your particular market outlook for Amerada Hess. If you are very bearish, you may want

Exhibit 9–2
Alternate put option hedge positions with 200 shares of Amerada Hess convertible preferred (from Exhibit 7–3)

	15	20	25	30	35
Stock price at expiration	15	20	25	30	35
Estimated convertible price	47	51	57	67	77
Buy two puts (investment = $11,780)					
Profit or (loss)—preferred	(2,000)	(1,200)	0	2,000	4,000
—puts	1,650	650	(350)	(350)	(350)
Dividends for six months	350	350	350	350	350
Commissions	(100)	(80)	(30)	(30)	(30)
Net profit or (loss)	(100)	(280)	(30)	1,970	3,970
Percent return—six months	−0.8	−2.4	−0.2	+16.7	+33.7
—annualized	−1.6	−4.8	−0.4	+33.4	+67.4
Expected profit = +12.1%*					
Buy three puts (investment = $11,965)					
Profit or (loss)—preferred	(2,000)	(1,200)	0	2,000	4,000
—puts	2,475	975	(525)	(525)	(525)
Dividends for six months	350	350	350	350	350
Commissions	(120)	(100)	(40)	(40)	(40)
Net profit or (loss)	705	25	(215)	1,785	3,785
Percent return—six months	+ 5.9	+0.2	−1.8	+14.9	+31.6
—annualized	+11.8	+0.4	−3.6	+29.8	+63.2
Expected profit = +12.4%*					
Buy four puts (investment = $12,150)					
Profit or (loss)—preferred	(2,000)	(1,200)	0	2,000	4,000
—puts	3,300	1,300	(700)	(700)	(700)
Dividends for six months	350	350	350	350	350
Commissions	(140)	(120)	(50)	(50)	(50)
Net profit or (loss)	1,510	330	(400)	1,600	3,600
Percent return—six months	+12.4	+2.7	−3.3	+13.2	+29.6
—annualized	+24.8	+5.4	−6.6	+26.4	+59.2
Expected profit = +12.1%*					

* Refer to Exhibit 9–1 for assumed stock price changes for calculating the expected profit.

to buy additional puts against the convertibles as an alternative to the outright short sale of the common stock. The purchase of 8 puts against 200 preferred, for example, offers about the same downside opportunity as shorting 400 common without exposing your investment capital to unlimited upside risk.

COMBINING PUTS AND CALLS WITH CONVERTIBLES

As I mentioned before and as shown by Exhibit 5–2 of Chapter 5, the purchase of a put and the sale of a call is like selling stock short. When done in conjunction with owning the stock, you have created a "short against the box." Yet, some stockbrokers actually recommend this strategy.

The risk/reward calculations are easy to perform as shown by Exhibit 9–3. The expected profit is only slightly more than the dividends paid on the stock and below that available from short-term money market instruments. So the logical question is, "Under what circumstances should puts be bought and calls sold?"

Exhibit 9–3
Amerada Hess—Common stock combined with puts and calls

Position
Buy 400 common stock at 25	= $10,000
Buy 4 Aug 25 puts at 1¾	= 700
Sell 4 Aug 25 calls at 2¼	= (900)
Commissions	= 100
Net investment	= $ 9,900

Risk/reward analysis

	15	20	25	30	35
Stock price at expiration	15	20	25	30	35
Put price at expiration	10	5	0	0	0
Call price at expiration	0	0	0	5	10
Profit or (loss)—stock	(4,000)	(2,000)	0	2,000	4,000
—puts	3,300	1,300	(700)	(700)	(700)
—calls	900	900	900	(1,100)	(3,100)
Dividends for six months	160	160	160	160	160
Commissions	(190)	(170)	(100)	(170)	(190)
Net profit or (loss)	170	190	260	190	170
Percent return—six months	+1.7	+1.9	+2.6	+1.9	+1.7
—annualized	+3.4	+3.8	+5.2	+3.8	+3.4

Probability analysis

Stock price change	Stock price	Probability		Annualized profit or loss		
+40%	$35	0.1	×	+3.4%	=	+0.34%
+20	30	0.2	×	+3.8	=	+0.76
0	25	0.4	×	+5.2	=	+2.08
−20	20	0.2	×	+3.8	=	+0.76
−40	15	0.1	×	+3.4	=	+0.34
Expected profit					=	+4.28%

Since a long put/short call combination is like selling short, we can create a traditional convertible/stock hedge similar to that presented by Exhibit 8–1 of Chapter 8, but with added advantages. The use of puts and calls for hedging undervalued convertibles *avoids* the dividends that must be paid on the traditional short sale of stock. And the normal difference in premiums between the two options will often equal or exceed the commission costs for their purchase and sale. Additionally, greater flexibility is available for shifting the risk/reward characteristics since different quantities of the puts and calls may be employed in the hedge.

Exhibit 9–4 illustrates three possible hedges of this type. The bullish and bearish positions are similar to the short sale of stock against convertibles per Chapter 8. The neutral hedge involves two puts and four calls. The two extra calls take part of the large upside potential of the bullish hedge and effectively spread it over the entire range of stock prices.

Exhibit 9–4
Alternate put and call option hedge positions with 200 shares of Amerada Hess convertible preferred (from Exhibit 7–3)

Stock price at expiration	15	20	25	30	35
Estimated convertible price	47	51	57	67	77
Bullish hedge—buy two puts and sell two calls (investment = $11,370)					
Profit or (loss)—preferred	(2,000)	(1,200)	0	2,000	4,000
—puts	1,650	650	(350)	(350)	(350)
—calls	450	450	450	(550)	(1,550)
Dividends for six months	350	350	350	350	350
Commissions	(130)	(110)	(70)	(110)	(130)
Net profit or (loss)	320	140	380	1,340	2,320
Percent return—six months	+2.8	+1.2	+3.3	+11.8	+20.4
—annualized	+5.6	+2.4	+6.6	+23.6	+40.8
Expected profit = +12.5%*					
Neutral hedge—buy two puts and sell four calls (investment = $10,760)					
Profit or (loss)—preferred	(2,000)	(1,200)	0	2,000	4,000
—puts	1,650	650	(350)	(350)	(350)
—calls	900	900	900	(1,100)	(3,100)
Dividends for six months	350	350	350	350	350
Commissions	(150)	(130)	(90)	(160)	(180)
Net profit or (loss)	750	570	810	740	720
Percent return—six months	+ 7.0	+ 5.3	+ 7.5	+ 6.9	+ 6.7
—annualized	+14.0	+10.6	+15.0	+13.8	+13.4
Expected profit = +13.6%*					
Bearish hedge—buy four puts and sell four calls (investment = $11,300)					
Profit or (loss)—preferred	(2,000)	(1,200)	0	2,000	4,000
—puts	3,300	1,300	(700)	(700)	(700)
—calls	900	900	900	(1,100)	(3,100)
Dividends for six months	350	350	350	350	350
Commissions	(190)	(170)	(100)	(170)	(190)
Net profit or (loss)	2,360	1,180	450	380	360
Percent return—six months	+20.9	+10.4	+4.0	+3.4	+3.2
—annualized	+41.8	+20.8	+8.0	+6.8	+6.4
Expected profit = +13.5%*					

* Refer to Exhibit 9–1 for assumed stock price changes for calculating the expected profit.

Again, the best choice of the three will depend on your market outlook as all positions offer high expected profits. The "superbear" may also buy additional puts for extra downside profits.

HEDGING ON MARGIN

As emphasized in prior chapters, margin in a conservative hedge program is regarded as a prudent investment tool. Exhibit 9–5 provides a detailed worksheet analysis of the neutral hedge from Exhibit 9–4. Full leverage is employed amounting to about 48 percent of the nonmargined hedge. As shown, the expected profit is increased to nearly 20 percent for any stock price at the options' expiration date.

In summary, the purchase of puts to protect undervalued convertibles is the only sensible strategy for employing listed put options with expectations for above average profits. Every other approach, whether it be buying, selling, or spreading, should be left to the speculators or floor traders. The following chapters will introduce the Superhedge™ strategies including bear market alternatives that include the purchase of put options.

Exhibit 9–5

WORK SHEET FOR EVALUATING PUT/CALL OPTION HEDGES

COMPANY *Amerada Hess*   DATE *February 1978*

DESCRIPTION OF SECURITIES

Convertible *$ 3.50 preferred*   Interest or Dividend Dates *Jan, Apr, Jul, Oct*

	Exer. Price	Expir. Month	Symbol	Value Line Rank	Value Line Volatility	Target Prices	Current Yield
Common Stock			AHC	4	110	25	3.2%
Convertible			AHC R	3	90	57	6.1
Put option	25	Aug	TE			1 3/4	
Call option	25	Aug	HE			2 1/4	

Conversion value = ___2.20___ shares x $ ___25.00___ per share = $ ___55.00___

Premium over conversion value = ___3.6___ %

Estimated investment value (per Value Line) = $ ___40.00___

Premium over investment value = ___42.5___ %

POSSIBLE· HEDGE POSITION: Bullish ___, Neutral _✔_, Bearish ___

Common stock:	___ at $ ___	= $ ___ + ___ comm.	= $ ___
Convertibles:	200 at $ 57	= $ 11400 + 160 comm.	= $ 11560
Puts bought:	2 at $ 175	= $ 350 + 35 comm.	= + 385
Calls sold:	4 at $ 225	= $ 900 − 55 comm.	= − 845
Net investment:	unleveraged		= $ 11100
	leveraged (*50% x 11560 + 385 − 845*)		= $ 5320

ESTIMATED PROFIT OR LOSS AT EXPIRATION DATE: unleveraged ___, leveraged _✔_

	Downside	Exercise Price(s)		Upside
Assumed stock price	15	25	30	35
Est. convertible price	47	57	67	77
Est. put price	10	0	0	0
Est. call price	0	0	5	10
Profit or (loss) - stock .... (	2000)	0	2000	4000
- conv .... (	1650)	(350)	(350)	(350)
- puts	900	900	(1100)	(3100)
- calls				
Income received	350	350	350	350
Margin interest at __8.0__ % .... (	230)	(230)	(230)	(230)
Commissions .... (	150)	(90)	(160)	(180)
Estimated gain or (loss)	520	580	510	490
Estimated return on investment	+ 9.8 %	+ 10.9 %	+ 9.6 %	+ 9.2 %
Annualized ROI (__.50__ years)	+ 19.5 %	+ 21.8 %	+ 19.2 %	+ 18.4 %

10

ADVANCED HEDGING STRATEGIES FOR THE MOST SOPHISTICATED INVESTOR

Hedging strategies utilizing convertible securities and options have always commanded the attention of sophisticated hedging specialists—those serious investors who searched out opportunities that offered advantages over all the rest of the stock market players. These traditional hedge techniques have been a source of extraordinary profits over the years, as illustrated by previous chapters.

However, it is becoming increasingly more difficult to find truly superior hedging situations in today's market of lower option premiums. Many more participants are now looking for those same opportunities that at one time were prevalent.

Several factors have contributed to the recent elevation of sophistication by the investment community.

1. The growth of the listed options market has introduced more and more investors to the concept of controlling risk by writing calls. Whether the risk-control is real or imaginary is not important. It's the increased use of options by "conservative" investors, believing they are managing their portfolios in a prudent manner, that has helped to depress premiums.

2. Advanced computer programs and inexpensive hand calculators

have helped to make it easier for investors to identify, evaluate, and execute option writing situations.

3. Regulatory authorities have modified their "prudent man" rules to permit the writing of covered call options and thereby opened the floodgates of institutional money to the selling side of the market.

4. Stockbrokers have seized on the popularity and mystique of option writing as a major source of commission income to replace the dying new issues market.

5. The market has been inundated with books and advisory services expounding the "fortunes" to be made by simply writing options.

Yes, the popularity of hedging with listed options has swelled in recent years. As a result, the options market has become relatively efficient and option premium levels have dropped. No longer does the option writer have an advantage over the buyer.

So, where do we go from here? Must we leave the game to the amateurs, or to the "experts" who manage the new option mutual funds or other institutional type call writing programs?

WHEN TO SELL CALL OPTIONS

Like the convertible securities market, there will *always* be pockets of inefficiency in the listed option market even if the overall option market is efficient. The reason for this is simply the day-to-day price fluctuations caused by unrelated supply/demand pressures between the stock market and the listed options market. For example, if a major institutional money manager decides to unload a large block of General Motors stock, there probably won't be concurrent and equal selling pressure on General Motors options. Experience indicates that options, like convertibles, tend to lag behind short-term price swings by their underlying common stocks. Eventually they catch up, but in the meantime the stock market creates selling (or buying) opportunities in the options market.

Therefore, we expect to always be able to find some overpriced call options to write, but the real art lies in being able to profit from these opportunities after all commission expenses. If every time we sell an overvalued call we must also purchase the underlying common stock, the hedge position will seldom be profitable after commissions on both sides of the trade. We must somehow devise a strategy that does not require frequent turnover of the long side of our portfolio; at the very least, the securities for the long side should be managed on their own merits—not arbitrarily purchased or sold because of a related option transaction.

THE SUPERHEDGE™ STRATEGY

Invented and implemented in 1975, the Superhedge™ strategy is the single most important breakthrough in the science of hedging with listed call options. This unique strategy goes well beyond the basic assumption that the two sides of a hedge must be directly related. The Superhedge™ strategy permits us to purchase the most undervalued securities available for the long side of our portfolio and to sell the most overpriced call options available for the short side.

If with sufficient diversification a portfolio is expected to perform like the market, then it should be possible to break the long and the short sides apart to create the ideal hedge portfolio; one employing the most undervalued and the most overvalued securities together with complete flexibility. This is in fact the case with the Superhedge™ strategy. With nearly three full years of established performance behind the concept, the results have been phenomenal.

When the Superhedge™ strategy was first developed, there was of course no track record. A large part of the credit for this new investment concept must go to Mr. Stanley Kritzik of Milwaukee, Wisconsin. He was responsible for conceptualizing and monitoring the Superhedge™ in its early stages.

Fortunately, Superhedge™ strategies are not available to most professional money managers because they are usually restricted to writing covered call options. Superhedge™ strategies are also unlikely to be employed by most individual investors because after only three years the concept is still both new and bold.

The following chapters will show how the Superhedge™ strategy has performed in the past and what can be expected of it in the future. But first, let's examine the concept of the prudent use of options in one's portfolio.

IS COVERED CALL WRITING REALLY PRUDENT?

Over the years, the practical application of prudent investing has confounded money managers and regulatory agencies alike. It is a complex subject having no quick and easy answers. For our purposes, we will assume that a diversified portfolio of typical common stocks is generally considered to be prudent for most investors. Against this yardstick, I will measure the alternatives.

Covered call writing is claimed to be conservative and prudent because it limits downside risk. I don't believe that it is necessarily prudent at all! Granted, the sale of a call option against common stock reduces risk to the extent of the premium received. But if most of the upside potential is given away, what good is it to *just reduce the risk?* Why not simply *eliminate the risk* altogether by placing your investment capital in treasury bills?

In reality, the sale of a covered call option actually *limits upside potential* while still exposing capital to most of the downside risk of the stock market—much like the naked sale of a put option (a tactic that is not yet considered to be prudent by the investment community).

In my opinion, the only prudent use of options (selling or buying) is in a strategy that offers *an above average expected profit.* But the sale of normally valued (or underpriced) calls against common stock in today's market does not meet the criteria. At one time it was a prudent strategy, but when premium levels are low as they are today, it cannot be considered prudent in my judgment. Yet, it was only recently that covered call writing was approved by the regulatory agencies for use by insurance companies, banks, and mutual funds. Their approvals were granted in spite of the existence of detailed probability studies showing that covered writing was likely to underperform the stock market.

Apparently, the regulators ignored these studies and used their own intuition or someone else's "track records." But remember, a poor strategy will actually produce superior performance results on occasion, as will the roll of the dice at a Las Vegas casino. So, any "track record" by itself may be totally unacceptable if it is unsupported by logic and good common sense. Anyone can devise a stock market system tailored to but a few years of market history that might fail miserably in the future.

I could go on but why bother. It's not my intention here to belittle the pillars of the investment community establishment any more than necessary in order to prove my point. Their "track record" speaks for itself. My objective is to give you the tools for outperforming the market with listed options, even when premiums are normally priced as I believe they are in today's market.

THE BASICS OF SUPERHEDGING™

For any hedging strategy to be successful, it *must* be based on the purchase of undervalued securities or the short sale of overpriced securities, or a combination of both. In fact, that is my definition of hedging. The sale of a normally valued security against another normally valued security is not a hedge by definition.

Consider, for example, someone who owns Ford Motor common stock. Is it wise to sell call options against the stock if the Ford calls are mathematically *underpriced* in the marketplace? Of course not! The sale of undervalued calls will just lock one into a losing investment posture over the long term. That is not hedging in my book.

But suppose that at the same time there were calls available on General Motors that were overpriced. Wouldn't it be better to sell overpriced calls on General Motors against the Ford common? Aren't these two automotive stocks expected to move up or down together most of the time?

Better yet, why not sell overpriced GM calls against the undervalued convertible bonds of Ford Motor illustrated in Chapter 4? Here we have a "hedge" position that offers a higher expected profit and is the first step towards building a Superhedge™ portfolio. I say first step because diversification becomes much more important with the Superhedge™ strategy than with traditional hedging. General Motors, for instance, could advance in price while Ford was declining.

So to further reduce risk, let us next buy the undervalued convertible preferred of Amerada Hess and select an overpriced call option to sell from the large group of oil companies having listed options (e.g., Tesoro Petroleum). If we repeat this process for ten or more situations, we will have a very well-diversified portfolio. In fact, it will be so well diversified that we can now consider breaking the industry ties within the portfolio (e.g., GM versus Ford and Amerada Hess versus Tesoro). Why not really search the marketplace and select *the* ten best convertibles for purchase and *the* ten most overpriced calls to sell? In fact, that is the basis for all of our Superhedge™ strategies. With the caveat that both sides of the hedge portfolio be diversified by both the number of different securities and by industry, the Superhedge™ strategy offers the best of all worlds, while in reality the two sides of the portfolio *are tied together by the overall stock market.*

The Superhedge™ concept permits the purchase of undervalued securities and the sale of overpriced securities. In addition, each side of the portfolio may also be managed independently for optimum performance. You may use whatever fundamental or technical tools you are comfortable with. My own techniques assume, as a starting point, that the underlying common stocks for both the long and the short sides will simply move as the market, and the risk/reward estimates in the following chapters are based on this efficient market concept. From a practical standpoint, I have used both fundamental and technical inputs that have modestly improved performance over the theoretical estimates to be presented.

The following chapters will demonstrate Superhedge™ alternatives for a bullish, neutral, or bearish posture. The long sides of the different portfolios will consist of undervalued dual-purpose funds or undervalued convertibles as discussed in Chapters 2 through 4. For each alternative strategy, we will assume a cash investment of $100,000, but this figure may be scaled up or down (within certain limitations) to fit individual investment needs.

The short sides of the alternate strategies will employ call options sold on $100,000 worth of underlying common stocks or multiples of this amount. To calculate probability estimates, we will assume that ten different options are sold on underlying stocks, each having a total market value of $10,000 (e.g., two options are sold on a $50 stock, five on a $20 stock, and so on).

THE SHORT SIDE OF THE SUPERHEDGE™ STRATEGIES

As will be shown, the different Superhedge™ strategies employ call options ranging from at-the-money to 10 percent out-of-the-money (or more). We will assume, for ease of illustration, that six-month calls are sold and that no transactions are made during the six-month period. Options ending up out-of-the-money will be allowed to expire worthless while those in-the-money will be bought back at their intrinsic value.

Exhibit 10–1 presents my profit and loss estimates for the call option side of the portfolios, assuming six-month market moves of between minus 20 percent to plus 20 percent. Price distributions for the underlying common stocks are the same as those used for evaluating convertibles in Chapter 4 (refer to Exhibit 4–5). Round-trip commissions for the initial sales and for repurchasing options having value at expiration are included for meaningful estimates.

Please study Exhibit 10–1 carefully, as I will refer to it often in the next chapters.

Exhibit 10–1
Probability analysis for ten different six-month calls, each sold on $10,000 worth of stock (at the exercise price) having average price volatility

Market move	Stock move	Number calls	8.0% premium at-the-money		5.5% premium 5% out-of-the-money		3.5% premium 10% out-of-the-money	
			Premium $	Weighted	Premium $	Weighted	Premium $	Weighted
+20%	+40%	1	(3,200)	(3,200)	(2,750)	(2,750)	(2,250)	(2,250)
	+30	2	(2,200)	(4,400)	(1,800)	(3,600)	(1,350)	(2,700)
	+20	4	(1,200)	(4,800)	(850)	(3,400)	(450)	(1,800)
	+10	2	(200)	(400)	100	200	350	700
	0	1	800	800	550	550	350	350
				(12,000)		(9,000)		(5,700)
Commissions				(1,300)		(1,150)		(1,000)
Profit or (loss)				(13,300)		(10,150)		(6,700)
+10%	+30%	1	(2,200)	(2,200)	(1,800)	(1,800)	(1,350)	(1,350)
	+20	2	(1,200)	(2,400)	(850)	(1,700)	(450)	(900)
	+10	4	(200)	(800)	100	400	350	1,400
	0	2	800	1,600	550	1,100	350	700
	-10	1	800	800	550	550	350	350
				(3,000)		(1,450)		200
Commissions				(1,050)		(950)		(800)
Profit or (loss)				(4,050)		(2,400)		(600)
0%	+20%	1	(1,200)	(1,200)	(850)	(850)	(450)	(450)
	+10	2	(200)	(400)	100	200	350	700
	0	4	800	3,200	550	2,200	350	1,400
	-10	2	800	1,600	550	1,100	350	700
	-20	1	800	800	550	550	350	350
				4,000		3,200		2,700
Commissions				(800)		(700)		(600)
Profit or (loss)				3,200		2,500		2,100

Exhibit 10–1 (continued)

Market move	Stock move	Number calls	8.0% premium at-the-money		5.5% premium 5% out-of-the-money		3.5% premium 10% out-of-the-money	
			Premium $	Weighted	Premium $	Weighted	Premium $	Weighted
−10%	+10%	1	(200)	(200)	100	100	350	350
	0	2	800	1,600	550	1,100	350	700
	−10	4	800	3,200	550	2,200	350	1,400
	−20	2	800	1,600	550	1,100	350	700
	−30	1	800	800	550	550	350	350
				7,000		5,050		3,500
Commissions				(650)		(600)		(500)
Profit or (loss)				6,350		4,450		3,000
−20%	0%	1	800	800	550	550	350	350
	−10	2	800	1,600	550	1,100	350	700
	−20	4	800	3,200	550	2,200	350	1,400
	−30	2	800	1,600	550	1,100	350	700
	−40	1	800	800	550	550	350	350
				8,000		5,500		3,500
Commissions				(600)		(550)		(500)
Profit or (loss)				7,400		4,950		3,000

Exhibit 10–2 presents my general guidelines for selecting the Superhedge™ call options. For estimating purposes I assume that the calls selected are held until expiration. In actual practice, however, an aggressively managed option portfolio should improve overall performance.

Exhibit 10–2
General guides for selecting Superhedge™ call options

1. Sell ten or more different call options on stocks in different industries.
2. Sell calls on stocks having close to average price volatility. If you do sell calls on a high volatility stock, the position size should be reduced accordingly.
3. Sell only those calls that are at least normally valued, and preferably, those that are overpriced.
4. Sell at-the-money or out-of-the-money calls as indicated for the selected strategy.
5. Sell calls having six months or more to expiration for maximum downside protection and lower commissions.
6. Sell calls on stocks that you believe will underperform the market if you employ short-term technical or fundamental analysis.

SUPERHEDGE™ I — A DYNAMIC BULL MARKET STRATEGY

Investment objective: To achieve a very high rate of return during sideways and advancing markets while limiting downside risk to less than that of a typical portfolio of common stocks.

Strategy: Long dual-purpose funds.
Short call options.

Net investment: $100,000.

THE LONG SIDE OF THE HEDGE PORTFOLIO

The long side of the SUPERHEDGE™ I portfolio consists of the most undervalued dual-purpose fund capital shares, as discussed in Chapter 3. I have chosen Gemini Fund for illustrating the strategy since it offers an outstanding risk/reward relationship with less downside risk than the other funds. Also, its performance over the years has been superb. Other funds having high risk/reward ratios may also be used, or you may employ two or more different funds for increased diversification.

During the latter months of 1977 and the early months of 1978, Gemini shares were trading at about $18 and represented $36 worth of underlying common stock. Assuming the purchase of 6,000 shares for $108,000, these capital shares controlled over $200,000 worth of fully diversified stock market equity.

THE SHORT SIDE OF THE HEDGE PORTFOLIO

Against the Gemini Fund capital shares, a diversified portfolio of about 20 different call options, trading at 5 to 10 percent out-of-the-money, will be sold on $200,000 worth of common stock. This essentially results in a covered call writing program on the market as both the long and short sides of the portfolio are broadly diversified.

For analytical purposes, I will assume that calls trading 5 percent out-of-the-money (o-o-t-m) are sold on $100,000 worth of stock, and calls trading 10 percent o-o-t-m are also sold on $100,000 worth of underlying common stock. Premiums received will total about $8,000 net after commissions.

The cost of the Gemini capital shares ($108,000) minus the call premiums received ($8,000) equals the net investment of $100,000. No debit balance is created by the position since the premiums are credited to the account. They are not frozen against you as in conventional short selling.

MARGIN REQUIREMENTS

Since the naked call options must be collateralized by the loan value of the capital shares, it is important to verify that federal margin requirements are satisfied before establishing the hedge portfolio. The calculations are as follows:

Gemini capital shares: $108,000 × 50%	= $54,000
Call options at 5% o-o-t-m: $95,000 × 30%	= 28,500
Call options at 10% o-o-t-m: $90,000 × 30%	= 27,000
Minus amount out-of-the-money	= −15,000
Minus net premiums received	= − 8,000
Minimum required investment	= $86,500

Notice that initial requirements fully margined ($86,500) are less than the net investment on a cash basis ($100,000). This leaves a cushion that provides the surplus collateral needed if the market rises sharply and stock prices underlying the uncovered calls advance toward the exercise prices of their calls. In addition, most brokerage houses will allow 70 percent of the capital share market value (which should be rising also) to provide for maintenance margin.

RISK/REWARD ANALYSIS

Exhibit 11–1 presents my risk/reward calculations for SUPERHEDGE™ I assuming the overall stock market trades within a range of between minus 20 percent and plus 20 percent over a six-month period.

Exhibit 11–1
SUPERHEDGE™ I

Position

Buy 6,000 Gemini capital shares at 18	= $108,000
Sell calls 5% o-o-t-m on $100,000	= (5,000)
Sell calls 10% o-o-t-m on $100,000	= (3,000)
Net investment	= $100,000

Risk/reward analysis

Estimated performance for a six-month market move of:

	−20%	−10%	0%	+10%	+20%
Profit or (loss)—Gemini	(25,000)	(10,000)	3,000	17,000	31,000
—calls	8,000	7,500	4,500	(3,000)	(17,000)
Net profit or (loss)	(17,000)	(2,500)	7,500	14,000	14,000
Percent return—six months	−17.0	−2.5	+ 7.5	+14.0	+14.0
—annualized	−34.0	−5.0	+15.0	+28.0	+28.0

Probability analysis

Market price change	Probability		Annualized profit or loss		
+20%	0.1	X	+28.0%	=	+ 2.8%
+10	0.2	X	+28.0	=	+ 5.6
0	0.4	X	+15.0	=	+ 6.0
−10	0.2	X	− 5.0	=	− 1.0
−20	0.1	X	−34.0	=	− 3.4
Expected profit				=	+10.0%

The profit and loss estimates for the Gemini capital shares are based on my assumptions that the securities held in their portfolio will move as the market, along with projected discount relationships. The profit and loss estimates for the naked call options are taken directly from Exhibit 10–1 of Chapter 10 by combining the estimates for 5 percent out-of-the-money and 10 percent out-of-the-money.

As shown by Exhibit 11–1, SUPERHEDGE™ I is an excellent alternative to the typical portfolio of common stocks. It offers very high rates of return during sideways and advancing markets at limited downside risk. In fact, the overall stock market must decline by about 20 percent during a brief six-month period before the strategy's risk begins to equal that of an unhedged stock portfolio.

The probability analysis of Exhibit 11–1 confirms that the SUPER-HEDGE™ I strategy is superior to conventional stock market portfolios by indicating a 10 percent expected profit.

A TWO-YEAR TRACK RECORD FOR SUPERHEDGE™ I

SUPERHEDGE™ I was implemented in July 1975 and published later in *How the Experts Beat the Market.* During its first year of operation to July 1976, the strategy returned about 60 percent on invested capital. During its second year to July 1977, it returned about 40 percent. In the latter half of 1977, most of my clients who employed the concept shifted their investment funds into other hedging strategies offering superior risk/reward opportunities.

SUPERHEDGE™ I still offers excellent performance potential for investors who are bullish on the market although it is not as exciting as when it was first introduced nearly three years ago. This is due to a narrowing of the dual-purpose fund discounts from their net asset values, the reduced leverage of the funds, and the decline in option premium levels.

The following chapters will present new Superhedge™ strategies that offer even greater expected profits for today's stock market.

12

SUPERHEDGE™ II —
A LOW-RISK BULL
MARKET STRATEGY

Investment objective: To achieve a high rate of return during sideways and advancing markets without losing money during declining
markets.

Strategy: Long undervalued convertibles.
Short call options.

Net investment: $100,000.

THE EVOLUTION OF SUPERHEDGE™ II

In Chapter 7 I demonstrated the advantages of selling covered call options against undervalued convertibles as compared to common stocks.
This has been a superb strategy in the past and still offers frequent opportunities for seeking above average investment returns. But as good
as this strategy has been in the past, I must, unfortunately, also report
the bad news. Option writers are catching on to this strategy. I believe
we're seeing a trend developing where more and more writers are
searching out the undervalued convertible. If I am right, we can expect
those undervalued convertibles having listed call options to be bid up
in price toward their normal values. We can also expect the additional
selling pressure on their related options to maintain their premiums at
normal or even below normal values. The efficient market is at work
again.

The answer to this problem is SUPERHEDGE™ II. Since we know that undervalued convertibles offer substantial advantages for the long side of any portfolio and that overpriced call options are superior securities for the short side, why not simply:

1. Buy the *best* undervalued convertibles that the market has to offer, and
2. Sell the most overvalued call options against them *without regard for tying the two sides of the hedge portfolio together!*

This strategy has been termed SUPERHEDGE™ II, and I believe it to be one of the most effective ways to achieve above average performance in today's stock market.

THE LONG SIDE OF THE HEDGE PORTFOLIO

The long side of the SUPERHEDGE™ II portfolio consists of undervalued convertible bonds and preferreds as shown in Chapter 4. Their total market value of about $107,500 is made up of 12 different convertibles in 10 bond units averaging about $9,000 for each position (or the appropriate number of preferred shares totaling $9,000 each).

THE SHORT SIDE OF THE HEDGE PORTFOLIO

To provide protection against a declining market, a diversified portfolio of at-the-money call options will be sold against $100,000 worth of underlying common stocks. As in SUPERHEDGE™ I, this essentially results in a covered writing program on the market. Premiums will total about $7,500 for a net cash investment of $100,000.

MARGIN REQUIREMENTS

Again, the naked call options are collateralized by the 50-percent loan value of the convertible securities held long. Federal margin requirements are calculated as follows:

Convertibles: $107,500 × 50%	=	$53,750
Call options at-the-money: $100,000 × 30%	=	30,000
Minus amount out-of-the-money	= −	0
Minus net premiums received	= −	7,500
Minimum required investment	=	$76,250

The initial margin requirement of $76,250 provides a substantial cushion against a sharply advancing market. Also, most brokerage firms will allow 70 percent of the market values of the convertibles for maintenance purposes.

RISK/REWARD ANALYSIS

Exhibit 12–1 presents the risk/reward calculations for SUPERHEDGE™ II for six-month market movements of between minus 20 percent and plus 20 percent.

Exhibit 12–1
SUPERHEDGE™ II

Position
Buy undervalued convertibles	= $107,500
Sell calls at-the-money on $100,000	= (7,500)
Net investment	= $100,000

Risk/reward analysis

Estimated performance for a six-month market move of:

	−20%	−10%	0%	+10%	+20%
Profit or (loss)—convertibles	(9,500)	(4,500)	1,000	7,500	16,000
—calls	7,500	6,500	3,000	(4,000)	(13,500)
Interest and dividends	3,500	3,500	3,500	3,500	3,500
Net profit or (loss)	1,500	5,500	7,500	7,000	6,000
Percent return—six months	+1.5	+ 5.5	+ 7.5	+ 7.0	+ 6.0
—annualized	+3.0	+11.0	+15.0	+14.0	+12.0

Probability analysis

Market price change	Probability		Annualized profit or loss		
+20%	0.1	×	+12.0%	=	+ 1.2%
+10	0.2	×	+14.0	=	+ 2.8
0	0.4	×	+15.0	=	+ 6.0
−10	0.2	×	+11.0	=	+ 2.2
−20	0.1	×	+ 3.0	=	+ 0.3
Expected profit				=	+12.5%

The profit and loss estimates for the convertibles held long are based on the analysis of Chapter 4 (Exhibits 4–4 and 4–5). The estimates for the naked call option portfolio are from Exhibit 10–1 of Chapter 10 for at-the-money calls.

SUPERHEDGE™ II, as shown by Exhibit 12–1, provides a very low-risk opportunity for achieving a high total return in sideways or advancing markets. In fact, even for a 20-percent market decline the strategy is still expected to be profitable.

The probability analysis of Exhibit 12–1 indicates a most satisfactory expected profit of 12.5 percent; 2.5 percentage points higher than for SUPERHEDGE™ I.

13

SUPERHEDGE™ III — A HIGH-PROFIT STRATEGY FOR NEUTRAL MARKETS

Investment objective: To achieve a very high rate of return during sideways markets without losing money during declining or advancing markets.

Strategy: Long undervalued convertibles.
Short call options (2:1 ratio).

Net investment: $100,000.

THE LONG SIDE OF THE HEDGE PORTFOLIO

The long side of a SUPERHEDGE™ III portfolio is the same as for SUPERHEDGE™ II; twelve different undervalued convertibles having a total market value of about $108,000.

THE SHORT SIDE OF THE HEDGE PORTFOLIO

To achieve a very high rate of return during sideways market movements, call options will be sold against $200,000 worth of underlying common stocks. This establishes a variable hedge position similar to the example for Amerada Hess in Chapter 7 (refer to Exhibit 7–9). As with the call options sold for SUPERHEDGE™ I, calls trading 5 percent o-o-t-m are sold on $100,000 worth of common stock, and calls trading

10 percent o-o-t-m are also sold on $100,000. Premiums received will total about $8,000 for a net cash investment of $100,000.

MARGIN REQUIREMENTS

As for all Superhedge™ strategies, the naked call options are collateralized by the loan value of the securities held long. Federal margin requirements are calculated as shown below.

Convertibles: $108,000 × 50%	=	$54,000
Call options at 5% o-o-t-m: $95,000 × 30%	=	28,500
Call options at 10% o-o-t-m: $90,000 × 30%	=	27,000
Minus amount out-of-the-money	=	−15,000
Minus net premiums received	=	− 8,000
Minimum required investment	=	$86,500

RISK/REWARD ANALYSIS

Risk/reward calculations are presented by Exhibit 13–1. As shown, SUPERHEDGE™ III offers a very high total return for those six-month

Exhibit 13–1
SUPERHEDGE™ III

Position
Buy undervalued convertibles	= $108,000
Sell calls 5% o-o-t-m on $100,000	= (5,000)
Sell calls 10% o-o-t-m on $100,000	= (3,000)
Net investment	= $100,000

Risk/reward analysis

Estimated performance for a six-month market move of:

	−20%	−10%	0%	+10%	+20%
Profit or (loss)—convertibles	(9,500)	(4,500)	1,000	7,500	16,000
—calls	8,000	7,500	4,500	(3,000)	(17,000)
Interest and dividends	3,500	3,500	3,500	3,500	3,500
Net profit or (loss)	2,000	6,500	9,000	8,000	2,500
Percent return—six months	+2.0	+ 6.5	+ 9.0	+ 8.0	+2.5
—annualized	+4.0	+13.0	+18.0	+16.0	+5.0

Probability analysis

Market price change	Probability		Annualized profit or loss		
+20%	0.1	×	+ 5.0%	=	+ 0.5%
+10	0.2	×	+16.0	=	+ 3.2
0	0.4	×	+18.0	=	+ 7.2
−10	0.2	×	+13.0	=	+ 2.6
−20	0.1	×	+ 4.0	=	+ 0.4
Expected profit				=	+13.9%

periods when the stock market trades within a range of plus or minus 10 percent. For those infrequent occasions when the market moves up or down by 20 percent, the strategy is still expected to be profitable.

The probability analysis of 13–1 confirms that SUPERHEDGE™ III is an outstanding strategy under most market conditions. The expected profit is nearly 14 percent!

A ONE-YEAR TRACK RECORD FOR SUPERHEDGE™ III

SUPERHEDGE™ III was developed and implemented during the latter days of 1976. My first client to employ the strategy earned a total net return of 30 percent during 1977 (during the first four months of 1978, the strategy has continued to perform at a 30-percent annualized rate). The 30-percent profit consisted of about 15 percent for both the long and short sides of the portfolio.

Why did the strategy perform so much better than was predicted for a year when the overall stock market declined by about 10 percent? Perhaps we experienced more good luck than bad, but the major reason lies in the fact that an actively managed hedge portfolio *should* outperform one that is passively managed (assumed for all of my risk/reward estimates).

14

SUPERHEDGE™ IV — AN ALTERNATIVE STRATEGY FOR NEUTRAL MARKETS

Investment objective: To achieve an above average rate of return under any stock market condition.

Strategy: Long undervalued convertibles.
Short stock and call options.

Net investment: $100,000.

THE LONG SIDE OF THE HEDGE PORTFOLIO

The long side of SUPERHEDGE™ IV consists of aggressive convertibles that qualify for the traditional hedge strategy of shorting common stock against them. This strategy was covered in Chapter 8. I will again assume that 12 different convertibles are purchased in 10 bond units with a total market value of $104,000.

THE SHORT SIDE OF THE HEDGE PORTFOLIO

The short side of the portfolio includes both common stock and naked call options. Stocks are sold short that are directly related to their underlying convertibles. The number of shares shorted are selected to give each individual hedge a break-even posture in a declining market—like

139

the bullish hedge in LTV illustrated by the worksheet of Exhibit 8–3. The concurrent sale of naked call options, trading 5 to 10 percent out-of-the-money, against $100,000 worth of common stock, effectively shifts most of the upside potential of the traditional bullish hedge portfolio to a satisfactory profit for any stock market movement. Premiums received will total about $4,000 for a net cash investment of $100,000.

MARGIN REQUIREMENTS

Since the stocks sold short are against related convertibles, no extra margin is needed for the short sales. The naked call options are collateralized by the convertibles held long. Margin calculations are as follows:

Convertibles: $104,000 × 50%	= $52,000
Common stock sold short	= 0
Call options at 5% o-o-t-m: $47,500 × 30%	= 14,250
Call options at 10% o-o-t-m: $45,000 × 30%	= 13,500
Minus amount out-of-the-money	= − 7,500
Minus net premiums received	= − 4,000
Minimum required investment	= $68,250

RISK/REWARD ANALYSIS

The risk/reward calculations for SUPERHEDGE™ IV are presented by Exhibit 14–1. As shown, this strategy is expected to provide a total return of about 12 percent regardless of stock market movement.

Exhibit 14–1
SUPERHEDGE™ IV

Position	
Buy undervalued convertibles	= $104,000
Short related common stock	= *
Sell calls 5% o-o-t-m on $50,000	= (2,500)
Sell calls 10% o-o-t-m on $50,000	= (1,500)
Net investment	= $100,000

Risk/reward analysis

	Estimated performance for a six-month market move of:				
	−20%	−10%	0%	+10%	+20%
Profit or (loss)—hedges	0	0	1,000	5,000	12,000
—calls	4,000	3,500	2,500	(1,500)	(8,500)
Net interest and dividends	2,500	2,500	2,500	2,500	2,500
Net profit or (loss)	6,500	6,000	6,000	6,000	6,000
Percent return—six months	+ 6.5	+ 6.0	+ 6.0	+ 6.0	+ 6.0
—annualized	+13.0	+12.0	+12.0	+12.0	+12.0

Exhibit 14–1 (*continued*)
Probability analysis

Market price change	Probability		Annualized profit or loss		
+20%	0.1	×	+12.0%	=	+ 1.2%
+10	0.2	×	+12.0	=	+ 2.4
0	0.4	×	+12.0	=	+ 4.8
−10	0.2	×	+12.0	=	+ 2.4
−20	0.1	×	+13.0	=	+ 1.3
Expected profit				=	+12.1%

* No funds are required for the short sale of common stock against related convertible securities.

AN ALTERNATE SUPERHEDGE™ IV STRATEGY

By selling call options trading at-the-money instead of 5 to 10 percent out, those investors who are somewhat more bearish may increase their total return during a declining market as illustrated by SUPERHEDGE™ IVa of Exhibit 14–2. SUPERHEDGE™ IVa shifts some of the upside opportunity to the downside while still offering an expected profit of about 12 percent.

Exhibit 14–2
SUPERHEDGE™ IVa

Position
Buy undervalued convertibles	=	$107,500
Short related common stock	=	*
Sell calls at-the-money on $100,000	=	(7,500)
Net investment	=	$100,000

Risk/reward analysis

	Estimated performance for a six-month market move of:				
	−20%	−10%	0%	+10%	+20%
Profit or (loss)—hedges	0	0	1,000	5,000	12,000
—calls	7,500	6,500	3,000	(4,000)	(13,500)
Net interest and dividends	2,500	2,500	2,500	2,500	2,500
Net profit or (loss)	10,000	9,000	6,500	3,500	1,000
Percent return—six months	+10.0	+ 9.0	+ 6.5	+3.5	+1.0
—annualized	+20.0	+18.0	+13.0	+7.0	+2.0

Probability analysis

Market price change	Probability		Annualized profit or loss		
+20%	0.1	×	+ 4.0%	=	+ 0.4%
+10	0.2	×	+ 7.0	=	+ 1.4
0	0.4	×	+13.0	=	+ 5.2
−10	0.2	×	+18.0	=	+ 3.6
−20	0.1	×	+20.0	=	+ 2.0
Expected profit				=	+12.6%

* No funds are required for the short sale of common stock against related convertible securities.

15

SUPERHEDGE™ V — A CONSERVATIVE BEAR MARKET STRATEGY

Investment objective: To achieve a high rate of return during declining markets without losing money during advancing markets.

Strategy: Long undervalued convertibles and put options.
Short call options.

Net investment: $100,000.

SHIFTING A SUPERHEDGE™ STRATEGY TO THE DOWNSIDE

SUPERHEDGE™ V employs the long and short side instruments of SUPERHEDGE™ II along with the purchase of listed put options for greater downside profit potential. I will assume that six-month puts are purchased on ten different common stocks, trading at-the-money, for 6 percent premium. The probability analysis for this diversified portfolio of put options is presented by Exhibit 15–1.

THE LONG SIDE OF THE HEDGE PORTFOLIO

The long side of a SUPERHEDGE™ V portfolio consists of undervalued convertibles having a total market value of about $101,000. In addition, a portfolio of listed put options on $100,000 worth of underlying com-

Exhibit 15–1
Probability analysis for ten different six-month puts, each bought on
$10,000 worth of stock having average price volatility

Market move	Stock move	Number puts	6.0% premium at-the-money	
			Premium $	Weighted
+20%	+40%	1	(600)	(600)
	+30	2	(600)	(1,200)
	+20	4	(600)	(2,400)
	+10	2	(600)	(1,200)
	0	1	(600)	(600)
				(6,000)
Commissions				(550)
Profit or (loss)				(6,550)
+10%	+30%	1	(600)	(600)
	+20	2	(600)	(1,200)
	+10	4	(600)	(2,400)
	0	2	(600)	(1,200)
	−10	1	400	400
				(5,000)
Commissions				(600)
Profit or (loss)				(5,600)
0%	+20%	1	(600)	(600)
	+10	2	(600)	(1,200)
	0	4	(600)	(2,400)
	−10	2	400	800
	−20	1	1,400	1,400
				(2,000)
Commissions				(750)
Profit or (loss)				(2,750)
−10%	+10%	1	(600)	(600)
	0	2	(600)	(1,200)
	−10	4	400	1,600
	−20	2	1,400	2,800
	−30	1	2,400	2,400
				5,000
Commissions				(1,000)
Profit or (loss)				4,000
−20%	0%	1	(600)	(600)
	−10	2	400	800
	−20	4	1,400	5,600
	−30	2	2,400	4,800
	−40	1	3,400	3,400
				14,000
Commissions				(1,250)
Profit or (loss)				12,750

mon stocks is established at a cost of $6,500 (including commissions). Total cost for the long side is $107,500.

THE SHORT SIDE OF THE HEDGE PORTFOLIO

Call options trading at-the-money are sold on $100,000 worth of common stock. Premiums received will total about $7,500 for a net cash investment of $100,000.

MARGIN REQUIREMENTS

The puts must be purchased for cash and have no loan value. The naked call options are collateralized by the 50-percent loan value of the convertibles. Federal margin requirements are calculated as follows:

Convertibles: $101,000 × 50%	=	$50,500
Put options: $6,500 × 100%	=	6,500
Call options at-the-money: $100,000 × 30%	=	30,000
Minus amount out-of-the-money	= −	0
Minus net call premiums received	= −	7,500
Minimum required investment	=	$79,500

RISK/REWARD ANALYSIS

Exhibit 15–2 presents the risk/reward calculations for SUPERHEDGE™ V. As shown, this strategy offers a high rate of return during sideways to lower markets without exposing capital to significant risk if the market moves higher than expected. The strategy is similar to the short sale of common stock against convertibles on a fully hedged basis except there is no liability for dividends on the shorted stock. Also, the higher premiums received for the calls sold over the premiums paid for the puts purchased provides additional profits.

The probability analysis of Exhibit 15–2 shows a satisfactory expected profit of 10.4 percent. Since the expected profit is lower than for the bullish or neutral strategies, SUPERHEDGE™ V should only be employed by those investors wanting a low-risk bear market investment posture.

Exhibit 15–2
SUPERHEDGE™ V

Position
  Buy undervalued convertibles   = $101,000
  Buy puts at-the-money on $100,000   =   6,500
  Sell calls at-the-money on $100,000 = (7,500)

Net investment   = $100,000

Risk/reward analysis

Estimated performance for a six-month market move of:

	−20%	−10%	0%	+10%	+20%
Profit or (loss)—convertibles	(9,000)	(4,500)	1,000	7,000	15,000
—puts	12,500	4,000	(3,000)	(5,500)	(6,500)
—calls	7,500	6,500	3,000	(4,000)	(13,500)
Interest and dividends	3,500	3,500	3,500	3,500	3,500
Net profit or (loss)	14,500	9,500	4,500	1,000	(1,500)
Percent return—six months	+14.5	+ 9.5	+4.5	+1.0	−1.5
—annualized	+29.0	+19.0	+9.0	+2.0	−3.0

Probability analysis

Market price change	Probability		Annualized profit or loss		
+20%	0.1	×	− 3.0%	=	− 0.3%
+10	0.2	×	+ 2.0	=	+ 0.4
0	0.4	×	+ 9.0	=	+ 3.6
−10	0.2	×	+19.0	=	+ 3.8
−20	0.1	×	+29.0	=	+ 2.9
Expected profit				=	+10.4%

16

SUPERHEDGE™ VI — AN AGGRESSIVE BEAR MARKET STRATEGY

Investment objective: To achieve a very high rate of return during declining markets while limiting upside risk to less than that of a typical portfolio of common stocks sold short.

Strategy: Long undervalued convertibles and put options.
Short common stock and call options.

Net investment: $100,000.

THE LONG SIDE OF THE HEDGE PORTFOLIO

My final Superhedge™ strategy is designed for a very high bear market profit potential at limited risk if you are wrong on your market forecast. As an alternative to the outright short sale of stocks, it offers more return during sideways or declining markets at much less upside risk. The strategy is essentially the combination of SUPERHEDGE™ IVa and the purchase of listed put options as in SUPERHEDGE™ V.

The long side of the portfolio, therefore, consists of aggressive convertibles having a market value of $101,000 and listed put options on $100,000 worth of stocks costing $6,500. Total cost for the long side is $107,500.

THE SHORT SIDE OF THE HEDGE PORTFOLIO

The short side of the portfolio includes both common stock sold short and naked call options. The stocks shorted are directly related to their convertibles. A sufficient quantity is shorted to give each individual hedge a break-even posture on the downside. Call options trading at-the-money are sold on $100,000 worth of underlying stocks. Premiums received will total about $7,500 for a net cash investment of $100,000.

Exhibit 16–1
SUPERHEDGE™ VI

Position

Buy undervalued convertibles	=	$101,000
Short related common stock	=	*
Buy puts at-the-money on $100,000	=	6,500
Sell calls at-the-money on $100,000	= (	7,500)
Net investment	=	$100,000

Risk/reward analysis

	Estimated performance for a six-month market move of:				
	−20%	−10%	0%	+10%	+20%
Profit or (loss)—hedges	0	0	1,000	5,000	12,000
—puts	12,500	4,000	(3,000)	(5,500)	(6,500)
—calls	7,500	6,500	3,000	(4,000)	(13,500)
Net interest and dividends	2,500	2,500	2,500	2,500	2,500
Net profit or (loss)	22,500	13,000	3,500	(2,000)	(5,500)
Percent return—six months	+22.5	+13.0	+3.5	−2.0	− 5.5
—annualized	+45.0	+26.0	+7.0	−4.0	−11.0

Probability analysis

Market price change	Probability		Annualized profit or loss		
+20%	0.1	×	−11.0%	=	− 1.1%
+10	0.2	×	− 4.0	=	− 0.8
0	0.4	×	+ 7.0	=	+ 2.8
−10	0.2	×	+26.0	=	+ 5.2
−20	0.1	×	+45.0	=	+ 4.5
Expected profit				=	+10.6%

* No funds are required for the short sale of common stock against related convertible securities.

MARGIN REQUIREMENTS

Convertibles: $101,000 × 50%	=	$50,500
Put options: $6,500 × 100%	=	6,500
Short related common stock	=	0
Call options at-the-money: $100,000 × 30%	=	30,000
Minus amount out-of-the-money	= −	0
Minus net call premiums received	= −	7,500
Minimum required investment	=	$79,500

RISK/REWARD ANALYSIS

Exhibit 16–1 shows that SUPERHEDGE™ VI offers a very high rate of return during declining markets at much less upside risk than the outright short sale of stocks. It also offers a satisfactory expected profit of 10.6 percent.

17

MANAGEMENT OF UNHEDGED PORTFOLIOS FOR PENSION FUNDS AND INDIVIDUAL INVESTORS

As I pointed out in the introductory chapter of this book, I have no solutions to the problems facing trustees of the *large* pension funds. Their overwhelming size makes it impossible for their managers to employ the strategies that are necessary for achieving above average market performance. Even the small to medium-size pension fund often cannot employ the more sophisticated strategies. The mechanical problems of safekeeping of securities, the use of put and call options, the short sale of stock, plus the lack of understanding by investment committee members can become major obstacles to utilizing advanced investment strategies.

The roller coaster ride many equity portfolios have been on in recent years is not what trustees of pension plans envision as prudent money management. And it is small consolation to match the Standard & Poor's 500 or the Dow Jones Industrial Average if the pension's assets have dropped over 10 percent as many did in 1977.

Many managers of pension funds will attempt to cushion the downside risk of an equity portfolio by keeping a major portion of their total assets in fixed income vehicles. The interest income from these fixed income investments will help to offset losses from the equity portion should the stock market decline. In advancing markets, the total assets *will not* match the market since only a portion of the assets are participating in the advance. Thus, the pension fund foresakes upside potential for downside safety.

Can this objective be met: participation in a bull market when it occurs while preserving capital during bear market declines? I feel strongly that the answer is *yes* for both small to medium pension funds and individual investors who employ undervalued convertible securities. As shown in Chapters 2 and 4, studies I have made and actual market experience to date indicate that a conservative investment objective for a managed portfolio of convertibles would be to match the market on the upside at one half the downside risk, and to provide a yield advantage over common stock portfolios.

As in any investment strategy, the frame of reference by which alternatives can be compared is the risk/reward analysis. Exhibit 17–1 compares these three investment alternatives:

A. Common stock portfolio (average volatility or index fund).
B. Balanced approach (50% common stocks and 50% fixed income).
C. Managed portfolio of convertible securities.

Exhibit 17–1
Investment alternatives

Investment alternatives	Possible stock price changes in twelve months				
	−20%	−10%	0%	+10%	+20%
A. Common stock* or index fund	−15.0%	−5.0%	+5.0%	+15.0%	+25.0%
B. 50% common stocks, 50% fixed income†	− 3.5	+1.5	+6.5	+11.5	+16.5
C. Managed convertible portfolio‡	− 3.5	+1.5	+6.5	+16.5	+26.5

Assumptions:
* Common stock yield = 5%.
† Fixed income yield = 8%.
‡ Convertible yield = 6½%.

The analysis of Exhibit 17–1 shows how these investment alternatives should react under various market conditions over the next twelve months. Since I am assuming an efficient stock market, I am not making a prediction of future stock market trends. Our objective is simply to participate in bull markets while preserving our capital during bear markets. If we can accomplish that objective, we should be able substantially to outperform the stock market over the long term.

Exhibit 17–1 shows that an investment in common stocks (alternative A) will act like the market since total assets are invested in common stocks. Much like the index funds and the large co-mingled bank funds, the equity fluctuation will be directly related to changes in the overall market. The more conservative approach, 50 percent common stocks and 50 percent fixed income (alternative B), will preserve some capital in declining markets with interest income offsetting losses from equity investments. But since only one half the assets are in equity investments, the total assets will not participate in an advancing stock market.

The risk/reward analysis of alternatives A and B indicates that neither offers advantages over the stock market.

A managed convertible portfolio (alternative C) offers significant advantages over alternatives A and B. In plan C, total assets participate in bull markets and provide the same downside safety factor as the balanced approach of alternative B. The analysis demonstrates why the use of undervalued convertibles would be the superior alternative and provide the best return on investment over the short term as well as the long run.

MANAGING A PORTFOLIO OF CONVERTIBLE SECURITIES

It is relatively easy to build a broadly diversified portfolio of undervalued convertibles, including representation in almost any industry one desires. About 500 actively traded convertibles (bonds and preferreds) are listed on the New York Stock Exchange. From this large group, a portfolio manager can usually find about 100 different convertibles that offer superior risk/reward characteristics compared to their underlying common stocks. Following are guidelines for buying and selling convertibles within the framework of an actively managed convertible portfolio.

Guidelines for buying convertibles

At this point you may wish to refer back to Chapter 4 for specific guidelines and selection procedures. The following are broad selection parameters.

Determine your investment objective relative to the stock market, e.g., an aggressive or conservative risk posture.

Select convertibles on good quality stocks. The convertibles should be undervalued and trading close to their conversion value—but not too far above their investment "floor." Remember that the investment value or floor is the convertible's worth without its conversion privilege, based primarily on current interest rates and investment quality. Therefore, built into the convertible portfolio is an investment floor which acts very much like the fixed income portion of alternative B in down markets.

Avoid convertibles trading at a premium over conversion value if they are well above their call prices. You will lose any conversion premium if they are called for redemption by the company.

Guidelines for selling convertibles

The selection process is based on logic and arithmetic, and the selling guidelines are also based on the same reasoning. Your entire portfolio should be for sale every day the market is open, provided, of course, that someone wants to pay you a fair market value. Here is the action you should take under different stock market conditions.

Advancing markets.   Sell when the convertible advances well above its investment floor since at this price level it will no longer offer the limited downside risk you want.

Sideways markets.   Sell if the convertible becomes overvalued, or even normally valued if you have an undervalued alternative available for replacement.

Declining markets: Sell when the convertible develops a sizable premium over conversion value as it will no longer participate as desired if the stock advances.

These buy and sell guidelines will allow you to protect the profits accumulated during the advancing stage of the market while limiting the risk of the overall portfolio. Over a market cycle, you should be able to outperform the stock market by five or more percentage points *annualized*. Exhibit 4–7 of Chapter 4 showed how a managed portfolio of convertibles beat the Standard & Poor's 500 by 30 percent during the 16-month period beginning in December 1976. The manager of the small to medium-sized pension fund can achieve above average market performance for the fund while still maintaining a low-risk posture consistent with prudent money management.

PORTFOLIO MANAGEMENT FOR CONVERTIBLE HEDGERS

The serious investor seeks to control risk while earning an above average return on investment capital. The control of risk is precisely what hedging with convertibles can accomplish, and it is therefore consistent with the goals of the serious fiduciary or individual investor. This final chapter deals with portfolio management techniques when employing hedging strategies, whether they be used by pension fund trustees or sophisticated individuals.

WHEN TO START A CONVERTIBLE HEDGE PROGRAM

One of the most frequently asked questions is when to start a hedge program. There never seems to be a good time. If the market is going up, it may go higher; so why hedge? If the market is going down, many investors feel locked in; so they can't hedge now. For instance, investors may have reasoned at the end of 1976 when the current bear market began that it was not a good time to begin a hedge program because the overwhelming market sentiment at that time was bullish. If those investors held diversified portfolios of common stocks, more than likely they have experienced the same decline as the general stock averages. In other words, their capital has eroded some 15 to 20 percent (dividends included) since the beginning of the bear market 15 months ago.

Convertible hedgers, on the other hand, *who employed the most bull-ish strategies* over that same 15-month period not only preserved their original capital but actually *gained* 15 percent or more. Remember that bullish hedge strategies can offer the full upside potential of the stock market. Therefore, whatever event had occurred, a market rise as the investors had hoped for, or the market decline which actually happened, those investors would have been better off in a hedge program. They would now have about 40 percent more capital in the market in a bullish posture, while still awaiting a market rise. If the market now returns to its former highs, the hedge portfolios should show additional increases while the unhedged common stock portfolios are just getting back to even.

What about investors who were actually bearish when the market slide began in early 1977? What alternatives did they have? Fearing a market decline, they might have sold out and gone into a cash position or into long-term money market instruments. Or they might have taken no ac-tion at all, which means that their portfolios did not reflect their market outlook. This inconsistency is common among investors because they do not realize they do have alternatives between being bullish (long common stocks) or being bearish (getting out of the market completely). Conventional approaches to investing have become obsolete, and in-vestors must be able to use the sophisticated strategies available to them to compete successfully in the market.

How did investors who were bearish and employed neutral or bearish hedging strategies since December 1976, fare? SUPERHEDGE™ III is a strategy that might have been used during this period and, in fact, was employed by several of my clients. As I pointed out in Chapter 13, SU-PERHEDGE™ III returned 30 percent in 1977. And the strategy was still producing at that phenomenal rate of return through the first four months of 1978.

Thus, investors who employed convertible hedge strategies were able to design their portfolios to conform to their market outlook and were able to take advantage of the volatility of the market instead of falling victim to it. Their performance is reason enough to employ hedging strategies, but it should not be overlooked that the risk factor for hedged convertibles is substantially lower than for unhedged stocks.

The time to begin a convertible hedge program is now!

HOW TO START A CONVERTIBLE HEDGE PROGRAM

Here are some guidelines that may be helpful in your personal financial planning and in building a hedge program.

Mark your portfolio to the market. When determining the value of your current holdings, include all stock market equity investments that you have and evaluate them based on current market prices. Paper losses represent a real decline of equity as any pension fund trustee will verify. Don't become trapped into thinking that a loss isn't a loss until it is taken, as many investors do.

Determine the risk/reward of your portfolio. Using price volatility factors will give you a mathematical, nonbiased evaluation of the relative risk of your portfolio. Once this figure is obtained, you will have a realistic idea of the degree of risk you are assuming. A typical common stock portfolio has a risk/reward of one. It should decline or rise at about the same percentage rate as the market.

Decide whether your present portfolio is consistent with your market outlook. Holding common stocks is being bullish on the market. Writing covered call options against common stocks is also a bullish strategy. The strategies that you employ in the market should be consistent with your market outlook and the amount of risk you are willing and able to assume.

Compare your desired risk/reward posture to the available hedge strategies consistent with your market outlook. By restudying Chapters 7 through 16, you can select the best strategies available in today's market, given a specific market outlook. They are summarized by Exhibit 18–1 for your convenience. Evaluate the risk/reward characteristics of the available strategies and determine whether you will use margin to leverage your investments. Many hedge opportunities are available to obtain the same upside potential as a conventional common stock portfolio but at a small fraction of the downside risk.

Become comfortable with the various hedge strategies. Researching and executing convertible hedge positions requires special skills that are not normally available in typical brokerage firms. So, it's going to take time and effort on your part. An alternative to doing the work yourself is to hire a money manager who specializes in convertible hedging. Be extra careful in this area. Many money managers have be-

Exhibit 18–1
Stock market alternatives for convertible hedgers

Market outlook	Recommended strategy	Chapter references
Bullish ·	Bullish traditional hedges on margin	7, 8, and 9
	SUPERHEDGE™ I	11
Moderately bullish	Convertible/covered call hedges	7
	Bullish convertible/stock hedges	8
	Convertibles and puts	9
	SUPERHEDGE™ II	12
Neutral	Convertible/ratio call hedges	7
	Neutral convertible/stock hedges	8
	Convertibles and put/call hedges	9
	SUPERHEDGE™ III	13
	SUPERHEDGE™ IV	14
Moderately bearish	Bearish convertible/stock hedges	8
	Convertibles and put/call hedges	9
	SUPERHEDGE™ V	15
Bearish	Bearish traditional hedges on margin	7, 8, and 9
	SUPERHEDGE™ VI	16

gun writing call options against common stocks and therefore feel they are hedging. As indicated earlier, writing calls against common stock is a poor strategy, given the low premium level currently prevailing. Select a money manager who fully understands and utilizes the more sophisticated strategies that you have studied in this book.

Select a stockbroker to work with.   If you plan to do it all yourself, you should probably work with a discount broker as most full service brokerage firms will be unable to add any extra value for the higher commissions charged. If instead you work with a stockbroker who specializes in convertible hedge strategies, expect to pay full commissions. The value added by a knowledgeable broker should more than pay for the difference. Skillful order execution alone should make up the difference in addition to good research ideas and assistance in helping monitor your portfolio.

Systematically begin switching your current holdings into hedge positions.   The time to start a hedge program is now, whether you are bullish or bearish or in the market or out of the market. All funds committed to common stock investments should be switched into a convertible hedge program.

Plan frequently to monitor your hedge portfolio.   Most hedge portfolios can be managed either passively or aggressively, but an aggressive approach should more than compensate for the extra effort and extra brokerage commissions. Plan to evaluate your portfolio at least weekly. If action is indicated (e.g., a convertible has moved from undervalued to normally valued, or a call option is approaching its intrinsic value or expiration date), the specific position should be monitored more closely. Avoid having your call options exercised against you as the commissions charged will be based on a round-trip trade on the higher priced underlying common stock. If you can, place some of the monitoring responsibility on your stockbroker's shoulders. At the very least, you should receive a sizable commission discount for an unwelcome exercise of a call option.

Determine the equity in your account quarterly. Knowing the bottom line is how you keep score. But even more important is the measurement of your performance against both your investment objective and the action of the market. If you are in a bullish strategy, for example, and neither the market nor your portfolio has done much, don't be disappointed and pull out. Your day will come and your patience will ultimately be rewarded.

Subscribe to one or more investment advisory services that specialize in convertible hedging. This is an absolute must as you will not have the time to research all the available opportunities and to develop new strategies as market conditions change. The three that I can recommend are:

Value Line Options and Convertibles: 5 East 44th St., New York, N.Y. 10017. A weekly service providing extensive data and articles relating to convertibles, warrants, and options. The data alone makes this service a must for anyone employing convertibles or convertible hedge strategies.

Systems and Forecasts: P.O. Box 1227, Old Village Station, Great Neck, N.Y. 11023. A biweekly service which specializes in the areas of market timing, convertibles, and traditional hedge strategies.

Advanced Investment Strategies: Thomas C. Noddings & Associates, Inc., 135 S. LaSalle St., Chicago, Ill. 60603. My own service, published monthly, specializes in convertibles, traditional hedges, and Superhedge™ strategies.

GLOSSARY

Accrued interest. Interest earned on a bond since its last interest payment date. The buyer of the bond pays the market price plus accrued interest to the seller and is entitled to the next interest payment in full. Exceptions include bonds in default and income bonds, which are traded flat (without accrued interest).

Adjusted exercise price. The warrant's exercise price divided by the number of shares receivable upon exercise. Where senior securities are usable at par in lieu of cash, the exercise price is first reduced by their discount below par to determine the effective exercise price. The effective exercise price is then divided by the number of shares to arrive at the adjusted exercise price.

Adjusted warrant price. The market price of the warrant divided by the number of shares receivable upon exercise.

Adjustment of conversion terms. Changes in conversion terms which may be provided for under the terms of the conversion privilege or by virtue of the implementation of an antidilution clause.

Antidilution clause. Provisions contained in most convertibles and warrants which call for the adjustment of the conversion or exercise terms in the event of stock splits, stock dividends, or the sale of new stock at a price below the conversion price of existing warrants or convertibles. In some cases, no adjustment is made for stock dividends under 5 percent in any single year.

Arbitrage. A simultaneous purchase and sale of identical or similar securities for an immediate profit upon conversion. This technique generally involves the purchase of a convertible bond or preferred that is trading at a price below its conversion value and the sale of its common stock.

Attached. Warrants are frequently attached to other securities, usually bonds. The security specifies the time and terms under which the warrants may be detached. The bonds and warrants may also trade individually or as units.

Bearer bond. A bond whose principal and interest are payable to its holder without specifying any name—the opposite of a registered bond.

161

Bond. A certificate of debt issued by a government, municipality, or corporation to the bondholder, whereby the issuer promises to pay interest on a regular basis and to repay the face amount of the bond on a specified date.

Bond indenture. The contract under which bonds are issued. It describes such terms of the agreement as interest rate, interest payment dates, date of maturity, redemption terms, conversion privileges, and the security for the loan.

Bond price quotation. Bonds are quoted as a percentage of par. Thus, 90 means 90 percent of a $1,000 bond, or $900. 110 means 110 percent of par or $1,100.

Break-even time. The time period in which a convertible bond or preferred will recapture the premium paid over conversion value through extra income when bond interest or preferred dividends exceed the common stock's dividend.

Buy back. Purchase transaction by which the writer of an option liquidates his position.

Call. An option giving the holder the right to purchase the stock from the seller of the contract at the specified price within a fixed period of time.

Call price. The amount of money a corporation is obliged to pay if it chooses to redeem its senior securities. In the case of bonds, the call price is usually expressed as a percentage of par. In the case of preferred stock, the call is the price per share. The call price normally starts somewhat above par and is reduced periodically.

Callable. Term applying to securities which contain a provision giving the issuer the right to retire the issue prior to its maturity date.

Capital gain or loss. A profit or loss from the sale of securities. A capital gain or loss may be either short term (less than one year) or long term (more than one year).

Change in terms. See "Adjustment of Conversion Terms."

Closed-end fund. An investment company having a fixed number of common shares outstanding and not having the obligation to redeem the shares at net asset value, as compared with a mutual fund. The market price of closed-end fund shares will fluctuate based on supply/demand conditions in the marketplace.

Common stock. Securities which represent an ownership interest in the corporation, also called "capital stock." Common stockholders assume greater risk than do preferred stockholders or bondholders, but generally exercise greater control and may gain the greater reward in the form of dividends and capital appreciation if the business is successful.

Conversion parity. Either the price at which common stock must sell for the market price of the convertible to equal its conversion value, or the price at which the convertible must sell for it to equal the current market value of the common shares to be received upon conversion. If the convertible is trading at a premium above conversion parity, it is generally better to sell the convertible and buy the stock rather than to convert.

Conversion ratio. The number of shares of common stock for which a convertible bond or preferred stock is exchangeable. For bonds, the ratio is normally expressed as the number of shares per $1,000 bond. For preferreds, the ratio is expressed as the number of shares per share of preferred stock.

Conversion value. The worth of a convertible bond or preferred if it were converted into common stock. It equals the number of shares to be received upon conversion times the current market price of the common. For a warrant, it equals the number of common stock shares per warrant times the current market price of the common, less the exercise price.

Convertible bond. A bond which may be exchanged, at the option of the holder, into common stock or other security in accordance with the terms of the bond indenture.

Convertible hedge. A market operation in which the investor buys or holds a convertible bond or preferred and sells call options or the common stock short against it.

Convertible preferred stock. An equity security, senior to the common stock, which may be exchanged, at the option of the holder, into common stock or other security in accordance with the terms of the conversion privilege.

Coupon bond. Bonds with coupons attached.

Coupons. Certificates attached to a bond which represent the right to periodic interest payments. The coupons are clipped as they become due and are deposited in a bank for payment.

Covered short sale. The short sale of common stock against a convertible.

Covered writer. Writer of a call option who owns the underlying stock or a convertible security.

Cum dividend. With the dividend.

Cumulative preferred. A preferred stock which provides for omitted dividends (arrearages) to be paid before dividends may be paid on the company's common stock.

Current yield. The yield on a bond figured by simply dividing the annual amount of interest by the current market price of the bond.

Debenture. A bond—an unsecured long-term certificate of debt issued by a corporation.

Debenture with warrants. A bond issue which has a specified number of warrants attached to each bond. Provisions are usually made for the detachment of the warrants after a specified date. See "Attached."

Debt security. A bond or note.

Default. Failure of the bond issuer to meet a contract obligation, such as payment of interest, maintenance of working capital requirements, or payment of principal via a sinking fund or at maturity.

Delayed convertibility. A convertible bond, preferred, or warrant which does not become convertible until some future date.

Dilution. The increase in the amount of common stock issued by a corporation due to conversion of warrants and convertibles. Dilution also refers to the issuing of additional common stock.

Discount. The amount by which a bond may be selling below its par value.

Effective exercise price. Where senior securities are usable at par in lieu of cash, the warrant's exercise price is reduced by the discount below par to determine the effective exercise price.

Equity. In a margin account, equity represents the difference between the market value of securities held in the account and the amount owed on them.

Ex-dividend. A stock trading without its current dividend. The seller of the stock on the ex-dividend date will receive the dividend.

Exercise. Surrendering a warrant or call option with the exercise price in exchange for the common stock. When a warrant is about to expire, or when terms are about to change, exercise may be mandatory. See "Forced Conversion."

Exercise price. Price at which the holder of a warrant or option may purchase or sell the underlying security upon exercise, sometimes called the striking price.

Expiration date. The date on which a conversion privilege ends. If the option or warrant has value, it must be exercised on or before the expiration date or it will become worthless.

Ex-warrants. Bonds trading without warrants attached.

Fabricated convertible. The combination of warrants plus bonds which are usable for exercise purposes at par value in lieu of cash is called a fabricated convertible and is equivalent to a regular convertible bond.

Flat. Bonds trading without accrued interest.

Forced conversion. When convertibles are called for redemption, or there is an adverse change in their conversion terms, or an upcoming expiration date, the holders of convertible securities may be forced to convert or to sell them to someone else who will convert. This is necessary to avoid a loss of value.

Guaranteed bond. A bond which includes a provision that the interest and principal will be paid by a company other than the debtor company in case of default.

Hedge. A position which includes securities which have been both purchased and sold short to take advantage of the price disparity between the related securities. See "Convertible Hedge."

Hypothecate. To pledge securities as collateral for a loan while still retaining ownership of the securities.

Income bond. A bond on which interest payments are contingent upon earnings.

Income preferred. A preferred stock on which dividend payments are contingent upon earnings.

Indenture. A contract or written agreement between a corporation and the holders of its securities, such as a bond indenture. See "Bond Indenture."

Interest rate. The cost of borrowing money determined by supply and demand and the nature of the loan.

Investment floor. The price at which a convertible bond or convertible preferred stock would not be expected to sell below upon a decline by the related common stock. See "Investment Value."

Investment value. The estimated value of a convertible bond or preferred stock without giving any consideration to its conversion privilege. Also known as the investment floor.

Leverage. Leverage is obtained by the use of borrowed money to finance a portion of one's investments or by the purchase of securities which contain inherent leverage such as warrants or call options. The use of leverage will normally amplify both potential profits and losses.

Life to expiration. The time remaining before a warrant or call option expires or before a conversion privilege expires.

Maintenance margin. Minimum equity requirements that must be maintained in a margin account as established by the New York Stock Exchange or the brokerage firm.

Margin. The amount of money and/or securities deposited with the brokerage firm to finance part of the cost of purchasing securities. The Federal Reserve Board establishes the minimum requirements through its Regulation T.

Margin account. An account with your brokerage firm in which securities are purchased on margin or in which securities are sold short.

Margin interest. The interest paid to the brokerage firm on the debit balance in the margin account.

Marking to the market. An adjustment to the credit balance in an account having securities sold short to reflect current market prices.

Mathematical advantage. The advantage offered by an undervalued convertible or warrant over purchase of its common stock. See "Risk/Reward Ratio."

Maturity date. A fixed date when the company must redeem a bond by paying the full face value to the bondholder.

Naked/Uncovered writer. Writer who does not own the underlying stock or convertible security.

Negative leverage. Leverage which exerts downward price pressure such as a convertible or warrant which is overpriced.

Normal value. A mathematically determined value for a convertible, option, or warrant in relationship to the current market value of the related common stock.

Normal value curve. A graphical representation of a convertible's, option's or warrant's normal value at any price level for the related common stock.

Option. A contract giving its holder the right to buy from or sell to another person a fixed amount of a certain stock at a specified price within a specified time. Listed options have time lengths up to nine months.

OTC. Over-the-counter, unlisted securities.

Overpriced convertible.   A convertible or warrant which is currently trading above its normal value.

Par.   The face value of a bond or preferred stock.

Parity.   See "Conversion Parity."

Plus cash.   A convertible bond or convertible preferred stock that requires an additional cash payment upon conversion.

Positive leverage.   Leverage which exerts upward price pressure such as a convertible or warrant which is undervalued.

Premium.   Price the buyer pays for the option and the price the writer receives for it.

Put.   A contract obligating the seller to take delivery of the stock and pay the specified price to the owner of the option within the time limit of the contract.

Redemption.   The act of retiring part or all of a bond issue prior to its maturity date. When a convertible bond issue is called by the issuing company and the bond is selling above the redemption price, it is equivalent to a forced conversion of the issue.

Registered bond.   A bond which is issued in the name of the holder as opposed to a bearer bond. If the bond is fully registered, or registered as to both principal and interest, interest is paid by check to the holder. Most recent issues of convertible bonds are fully registered.

Regulation T.   A Federal Reserve Board regulation which establishes the maximum amount of credit that brokers may extend to their customers for the purpose of buying securities on margin.

Regulation U.   A Federal Reserve Board regulation which establishes the maximum amount of credit that banks may advance to their customers for the purchase of securities.

Reverse warrant hedge.   The short sale of a warrant against the purchase of the related common stock or securities which are convertible into the common.

Right.   Usually refers to a short-term option to subscribe to a new issue of securities and is given by the company to existing stockholders.

Risk/Reward ratio.   A simple formula for determining whether a convertible or a warrant offers a mathematical advantage over its common stock. Assuming that the common will either rise or decline by 50 percent (other price movements may also be used) the risk/reward ratio for the convertible may be computed as follows:

$$\frac{\text{Risk/reward}}{\text{ratio}} = \frac{50\% \text{ stock decline}}{\% \text{ convertible decline}} \times \frac{\% \text{ convertible advance}}{50\% \text{ stock advance}}$$

A ratio in excess of 1.0 would indicate a positive advantage.

Securities.   Includes bonds, preferred stocks, common stocks, options, and warrants.

Senior securities.   Bonds or preferred stocks which have a prior claim over the common stock in the distribution of interest or dividends, or to assets in case of liquidation.

Senior securities usable at par value in lieu of cash. Securities usable at par value in lieu of cash when exercising a warrant. If the usable senior securities are selling below par, the warrant's exercise price is reduced by the percentage discount to determine the effective exercise price.

Short covering. The purchase of a security to return it to the lender to close out a prior short sale.

Short interest. The total amount of securities sold short in the market. A report is issued each month covering all issues on the New York and American Stock Exchanges in which there was a significant short position.

Short position. Securities sold short and not covered as of a particular date.

Short sale. The sale of a security which one does not own with the hope of buying it back at a lower price at some future time for a profit/or to protect a convertible against a market decline.

Short squeeze. A sharp increase in the price of a security as a result of panic short covering or difficulty in borrowing the security to maintain the short position (as in a tender offer).

Stock dividend. The issuance of small amounts of stock (usually 5 percent or less) in lieu of a cash dividend. This technique is normally employed by companies which desire to conserve cash for expansion or other purposes.

Subordinated. Subject to the prior claim of other senior securities and usually not secured by any specific property. Most convertible bonds are subordinate to regular bonds issued by the company.

Tangible value. See "Conversion Value."

Undervalued convertible. A convertible which is currently trading below its normal value.

Unit. A package of securities issued and traded in units such as bonds and warrants.

Up-tick. A term used to designate a transaction made at a price higher than the preceding transaction. Short sales may only be executed on an up-tick.

Warrant. A negotiable security issued by a company which represents a long-term option to purchase common stock from the company on specified terms.

Warrant agreement. A contract from the company or written agreement between a corporation and the holders of its warrants.

Warrant hedge. A market operation in which the investor buys or holds a warrant and sells call options or common stock short against it.

When detached. A form of "when issued" transaction when securities are issued as a package and are not separable for a period of time.

When issued. This term indicates a conditional transaction in a security which has been authorized for issuance but has not as yet been actually issued.

With warrants. Bonds quoted "ww" means that warrants are still attached and the price of the package includes both the bond and warrants.

Writer. Person creating the option, also known as the seller.

Yield. The dividends or interest paid annually by a company on a security, expressed as a percentage of the current market price of the security.

Yield to maturity. The effective yield of a bond, taking into account its premium or discount from par, if one were to hold it to maturity when it is expected to be redeemed by the company at par value.

INDEX